THE GUYS' GUIDE
TO SEPARATION AND DIVORCE

SIOBHAN MULLINS

# THE GUYS' GUIDE TO SEPARATION AND DIVORCE

THE WORLD'S MOST INSPIRING GUIDE TO GETTING THE MOST OUT OF LIFE AFTER THE MOST CHALLENGING DECISION OF YOUR LIFE.

SIOBHAN MULLINS

First published in 2022 by Dean Publishing
PO Box 119
Mt. Macedon, Victoria, 3441
Australia
deanpublishing.com

Copyright © Siobhan Mullins

All rights reserved. No part of this publication may be reproduced, stored in a retrieval system or transmitted in any way or by any means, electronic, mechanical, photocopying, recording or otherwise, without the prior written permission of the author.

Cataloguing-in-Publication Data
National Library of Australia
Title: The Guys' Guide to Divorce & Separation: The world's most inspiring guide to getting the most out of life after the most challenging decision of your life.
Edition: 1st edn
ISBN: 978-1-92545-255-6
Category: LAW / Family Law / Divorce & Separation

This publication is intended to be an information source only. It is sold on the basis of the terms and understanding that the publisher, author and editors are not responsible for any outcomes as a result of actions taken in purported reliance on any part of the publication, nor any error in, or omission, from this publication. The publisher, author and editors expressly disclaim all or any liability (including liability for negligence) and responsibility to any reader for the consequences, financial or otherwise, of anything done or omitted to be done by any ready in purported reliance on the material contained in this publication.

The commentary contained within this book on legislation, case law and any precedent contained within this book does not constitute legal advice or legal services and should not be relied on for that purpose or any related purpose. Any information and content in this book is general in nature only and does not take into account the objectives and needs of any particular person. Any reader should consult and take advice from a competent and suitably qualified professional regarding their own particular situation.

Dedication

To the man who told me to study law, John.

To my dad, for being an incredible father and role model.

To my parents, my brothers, and my partner,
who have helped me heal.

To Paul Dunn, who has helped shape Separate Together
(and me) into what it has become.

A special thanks must go to my dearest friend and
colleague, Lucy. Your unwavering support has meant,
and continues to mean, so much to me.

Contents

INTRODUCTION 9
Definitions & Terms 17

CHAPTER 1 – GETTING THE LAY OF THE LAND 23
Introduction 25
What Needs to Get Sorted 26
Interim Arrangements 29
Important Time Limits 50

CHAPTER 2 – LOOKING AFTER YOU 53
Grief Cycle 55
Alarming Stats & Facts........................... 59
Bad Health Contributors 62
Managing the Relationship with Your Partner 71

CHAPTER 3 – PARENTING 79
Introduction 81
What the Law Says 82
Examples of Parenting Agreements 84
FAQs.. 91
Parenting Apps 104

CHAPTER 4 – CHILD SUPPORT 105
Introduction 107
What the Law Says 108
FAQs.. 109
Real Life Examples of Child Support Agreements .. 122

CHAPTER 5 – YOUR FINANCIAL SPLIT (PROPERTY SETTLEMENT) 125
Introduction 127
What the Law Says 128
Working Out the Financial Split 130
Real Life 131
Information Sharing 133
FAQs 134

CHAPTER 6 – MAINTENANCE 151
Introduction 153
What the Law Says 155
FAQs 157

CHAPTER 7 – DIVORCE 161
Introduction 163
FAQs 164

CHAPTER 8 – THINKING AHEAD 175
Introduction 177
Checklist 178

CHAPTER 9 – GETTING TO AN AGREEMENT 187
Introduction 189
Options to Agree 190
Making the Agreement Official 192

GUYS' EXPERIENCE 201

CONCLUSION 207

NOTE FOR HER 210

ABOUT THE AUTHOR 213

NOTES 214

ENDNOTES 218

Introduction

Who This Book is For

This book is for the everyday guy who's trying to work through the emotions and practical aspects of his separation: the financial, parenting and child support (as might be relevant) matters.

This book is for the guy who wants to do the right thing by achieving an outcome that satisfies his needs, his partner's, and his kids' so that he and his family can move forward with their lives. He loves his kids and wants regular time with them. He wants certainty as to his financial commitments to his partner and kids moving forward. Whilst he might find his partner or the situation frustrating, he doesn't hate his partner. He is disappointed, perhaps sad, but accepting – at least somewhat – of the break-up.

He is lost regarding where to start and how to move forward with the separation. He doesn't know what an appropriate outcome is for parenting, child support and finances. He doesn't fully understand his partner's emotions or how to best respond to her or manage their relationship.

He wants to avoid the stress, turmoil, uncertainty, and expense of involving lawyers or going to court.

He's not a big reader. He's not a big talker and doesn't really show emotion. He doesn't necessarily have anyone he can easily talk to or get advice from, but he wants quick, smart, practical real-life answers without complexity.

How This Book Will Help You

For this book, I interviewed male clients who I worked with during their separation. Many of these men said they didn't talk to their male friends about how they managed their split and their emotions. They agreed that they'd have found it useful to have some guy advice and insights on this topic. And so, I've included their advice and insights in this book.

By the end of this guide, you'll feel not only relief about having some of those burning questions answered, but inspired to move forward with your separation in a positive and constructive way, together with your partner.

This is a straighty-180 book. Right now, if you believe that 50/50 will be a fair financial split or that your child should live with you and your partner 50 percent of the time because that's what is "fair", by the end of this book, you'll know differently. You will get a reality check on what informs appropriate financial, child support and parenting arrangements after separation.

And, if you've ever wondered why your partner is behaving a certain way without reason (in your eyes), I'll share insights with you so you can better understand her perspective. This empathy will see you better respond to her and consequently help your relationship.

This is not a gender-bashing book or a flowery gender-championing book. This book is designed to help you get the lay of the land when it comes to the matters that you need to resolve and the principles that guide appropriate outcomes in the eyes of the law. This clarity, direction and understanding will not only empower you to feel confident moving forward, but also help you set realistic expectations. It means you'll be able to contextualise your partner's proposals or behaviours, as well as your own, with reality.

All of this is designed to steer you towards reaching a separation agreement with your partner about all matters relevant to you.

My Story

At the time of writing this, I'm a 32-year-old, female, collaboratively trained family lawyer and the founder of a Canberra-based, online multi award-winning family law firm, Separate Together. I've written a previous bestseller titled *Splitting Up Together: The How-To Handbook for an AMICABLE Divorce*, which breaks down from start to finish what's involved in separating and making it all official.

I've been a family lawyer since February 2013, and I used to do the whole traditional lawyering, going to court, attending mediations, and writing back and forth letters to other lawyers. I'd say I represented more dads at court than mums, and those dads who I did work with were, in my experience, positive male role models for their kids.

I've never married or experienced a separation. My passion and interest are in helping people through practical education and guidance in a unique and different way.

In the last five years, I've niched a space for myself, working with couples who are on talking terms, who have a separation agreement, who simply need help to sort the paperwork to make it all official. I've won industry awards for my "innovative" approach in family law. What I and the team do at Separate Together is fairly gender-neutral – we appeal to male and female genders 50/50. We're not seen as pro-female or pro-male.

It might seem at odds that I'm female and writing a book for men who are separating, but I have positive relationships with the males in my life, including my partner, my dad, my three brothers and extended male family members. I know the value and significance of healthy male relationships in my own life, and I want that for other couples and their kids.

So, I write this book and give guidance and information to any one of the important males in my life who I care for and want the best for.

Why I Wrote This Book

More needs to be done to bring attention to and support men's mental health, particularly in men who are experiencing separation.

The insights from men interviewed for this book highlight how little they shared with their male friends about their separation and how they felt. Statistics show that men have an increased likelihood of suffering a mental illness following the breakdown of their relationship.

This can impact all aspects of a man's life: his work performance, his physical health and overall wellbeing, his ability to parent in the way he aspires to, his relationship with his kids, his child's future, and more.

Without a reality check regarding appropriate parenting, financial, and child support outcomes in the eyes of the law, a person is limited in his/her/their ability to constructively engage and agree on these matters.

Compared to their female counterparts, men aren't the best at asking for help. The absence of male-specific information, resources, and support services can leave some men feeling disempowered, which can perpetuate the belief that the legal system is against them, discouraging them from getting legal help.

In not asking for help from professionals and not hearing from others' experiences, men can have unrealistic expectations regarding appropriate outcomes for parenting, child support, and financial matters after separating.

Without realistic expectations, how can an everyday guy meaningfully work with his partner to reach an agreement and make their separation official without legal intervention, without incurring significant cost, and without there being increased conflict between him and his partner? With the impacts of parental conflict being intergenerational, parents want to avoid inflicting irreparable damage on their children.

The reality is that the immediate priorities and challenges that the everyday guy faces after separating are somewhat different from those faced by women. In my experience, men and women are guaranteed to ask the same questions, just at different stages in the separation process.

I've written this with the everyday guy reader in mind; however, the beauty of this book is that the content is still just as relevant to women. So, if you're reading this and you believe that your partner might just benefit from this book, I encourage you to share it with her.

I intend for this book to be a contribution to helping separated men feel supported in their own set of specific challenges and questions.

Getting the Most Out of the Book

Read the full answers, not just the short answer.

I've made all chapter introductions barebones. Read these.

Get familiar with the definitions and terms section on page 17. It'll make reading this book much easier.

Disclaimer

- **Not legal advice.** This book isn't advice, and it isn't a replacement for legal advice from an experienced family lawyer on what you should do.

- **No offence intended.** What I've written reflects my nine years' plus worth of experience as a family lawyer and is based on my observations, learnings and insights into reading situations and people. I've made comments and shared my observations without intending to cause any offense against any gender.

- **You need to know THIS.** I'd say that I've observed family violence (at differing scales) with about half of the couples I work with, and I'd say that most of these people would be unfamiliar with the behaviours that I observed constituting the definition of family violence.

    I firmly believe it's important for you to familiarise yourself with the family violence definitions and behaviours. For two reasons:
    - You may be a survivor yourself. Family violence does tend to be perpetrated more by men towards women, but men suffer and experience this too from their partners. Family violence isn't all physical and as you familiarise yourself with the definition and the types of behaviour, you'll come to realise this too.
    - You don't want to be accused of perpetrating family violence towards your partner. By better understanding the behaviours that fall within the family violence definition, you can consciously and actively choose to behave in a different way that minimises the chances of your partner feeling intimidated, harassed, or threatened in some way and accusing you of family violence behaviours, in turn self-protecting.

- **Currency.** Everything written is accurate as of July 25th, 2022. Family law and our family law legal system structure underwent some not so insignificant changes in 2021, including the merging of two courts that dealt with family law matters.

- **Selling real estate.** If at the time you're reading this you and your partner agree to sell a property before making your financial separation agreement official, you really must get legal advice before. Aside from some potentially significant cost saving for you in stamp duty if you make your agreement official before exchanging on the sale contracts, you also need to protect the house sale proceeds. If the property is registered in your partner's sole name, then you may need to lodge what's called a "caveat" against the house. Get advice from an experienced family lawyer before it's too late.

- **Family violence allegations.** If there are allegations of family violence or there is a history of family violence, you should seek legal advice specific to your situation.

- **Court proceedings.** If there are proceedings before the court about matters relating to your separation, this guide isn't enough for you to rely on. Don't expect an in-depth explanation of the court process. You should get appropriate legal advice on what an appropriate outcome is for you and your family, and a strategy for resolving all separation matters. Be sure to get ongoing and updated legal advice.

- **References to law.** This is specific to the Family Law Act 1975 (Cth), which applies to almost all of Australia, the exception being Western Australia (although the legal principles are similar/the same).

Getting legal advice

- Community Legal Centre or your local Legal Aid. Simply google those words, and your state or territory and relevant organisations should appear.

- Collaborative family lawyers. Google "collaborative family lawyers" with your state or territory, and either your local jurisdiction's collaborative family law group website or various names of collaborative trained local family lawyers should appear.

- Free phone support. Call the Family Relationship Advice Line (1800 050 321) for advice and referrals to local services.

DEFINITIONS & TERMS

Adult child maintenance
Financial support for a child who is over the age of 18 years.

Centrelink
The government agency that delivers social security payments and services to Australians.

Child custody
An outdated term used to describe whom a child lives and spends time with.
   In 1996, our legislation was changed to remove these words, thereby alleviating the win-lose proposition regarding a child's care. Throughout this book, we call this "parenting."

Child support
Child support is financial support provided for a child.
   Child support can refer to regular (periodic) and irregular (non-periodic) financial support for a child.

Child Support Agency
The government agency that manages child support arrangements between separated parents.

Coercive control
"A pattern of domination that includes tactics to isolate, degrade, exploit and control" a person "as well as to frighten them or hurt them physically."[1]
   The use by one person of controlling and manipulative behaviours such as isolation, emotional manipulation, surveillance, psychological abuse and financial restriction against another person over a period of time for the purpose of establishing and maintaining control. In relationships characterised by coercive control, abusers use

tactics of fear and intimidation to exert power over their victim, undermining their independence and self-worth.[2]

Coercive control describes a tactical pattern of behaviours that are designed by the perpetrator to control, intimidate, create dependency, and render the victim powerless. The perpetrator will use a range of tactics to leverage the emotional investment the victim has in the relationship to introduce rules and regulations that only apply to the victim, as well as penalties for non-compliance.[3]

Equity

The term to describe the difference in your house's value and the amount you owe on it. For example, if your home is worth $450,000 and you owe -$150,000, then you have $300,000 equity. To work out the equity, you minus what you owe on the home loan from the home's value.

Family violence

"Family violence means violent, threatening or other behaviour by a person that coerces or controls a member of the person's family (the family member), or causes the family member to be fearful."[4] This is the definition under our Family Law Act 1975 (Cth).

Family violence isn't just physical abuse though. It can be any of the following behaviours, and both women and men can be victims and survivors of family violence:

- Threats of suicide or self-harm by you or your partner

- Deliberate and intentional damage to property – fists through walls, car scratching, breaking plates, smashing, or breaking personal belongings or furniture

- Sharing/distribution of intimate photos/videos/private content

- Assault – slapping, punching, choking, pinching, hitting

- Sexual violence towards you/your partner, including sex without consent, sexually abusive behaviour, pressure to participate in sex or sexual acts

- Stalking of you/your partner – following, GPS/phone tracking or unwanted contact

- Violation of your/your partner's privacy

- Emotional abuse towards you or your partner, including taunts, put downs, verbal abuse, shouting, yelling, and name calling

- Deliberately causing death or injury to an animal

- Threats of harm to you or your partner, pets, property, or children

- Financial control – unreasonably denying you or your partner the financial autonomy you/they would otherwise have and/or withholding financial support

- Preventing you or your partner from connecting or communicating with friends, family, or culture

- Depriving someone of their liberty and autonomy – for example, the freedom to leave the home

- Behaviours to pressure or persuade you or your partner to consent to acts or decisions

Gaslighting
Term used to describe psychologically abusive, manipulative behaviours designed to cause a person to doubt their own perception of events, memory, or sanity.

Maintenance
Maintenance is what the Americans term "alimony." It is the provision of financial support (or not) between a separated couple. For married couples, it's called "spouse maintenance." Note that maintenance is different from adult child maintenance and child maintenance

Mortgage
The lender's right to sell a property, which is used as security for the loan (funds borrowed), if the loan is defaulted.

Mortgage (home loan) repayments
A mortgage repayment isn't really a thing. Colloquially people say "pay the mortgage," but really it's "pay the home loan," which means to reduce the amount owing on the loan.

Partner
Your current or former spouse, your ex or former partner.

We say "partner" because for you to get through this process, you and she need to work together. It's a collaborative team effort that is about getting the best outcomes for you and your family.

Property settlement
This is the formal legal term used to describe the split of your and your partner's assets, debts, superannuation, and resources.

We keep this simple by calling it "financial split."

Services Australia
The government department that runs Medicare, Centrelink, and the Child Support Agency.

Sexual violence
"Sexual violence can include behaviours such as sexual harassment, stalking, forced or deceptive sexual exploitation (such as having images taken and/or distributed without freely given consent), indecent assault and rape."[5]

"Unwanted touching, sexual harassment and intimidation, coerced sexual activity, sexual assault and rape."[6]

Siobhan is sharing more in her INTERACTIVE book.

See exclusive downloads, videos, audios and photos.

DOWNLOAD it now at deanpublishing.com/siobhanmullins

CHAPTER 1

Getting the Lay of the Land

1
GETTING THE LAY OF THE LAND

DEFINITIONS & TERMS

INTRODUCTION

WHAT NEEDS TO GET SORTED

INTERIM ARRANGEMENTS

Should one of us move out of the family home?

Does anyone have to move out of the family home?

Can I change the locks to the home after my partner moves out?

Can my partner change the locks to the house after I move out?

How do I know if we're separated?

Can we be separated but living under the same roof?

Until we agree on a financial split, should we keep or change how we manage our finances and expenses?

Do I have to pay the home loan if I'm no longer living there?

Does my partner have to contribute to the home loan even though she's not living there?

Do I have to contribute to rent for the family home if I'm no longer living there?

What steps should I consider taking now to protect me/us financially until we agree on a financial split?

Should I tell my partner about these protective interim financial steps?

Do I have to pay child support if we're separated but living under the same roof?

When do we need to apply for a child support assessment?

Does it matter who applies for a child support assessment?

Do we have to apply for a child support assessment?

If I or my partner receive maintenance or formal child support, do we have to tell Centrelink?

Do we need to do anything formal about our child's care?

Can my partner stop me from seeing our kids?

Can I stop my partner from seeing our kids?

What should I do if my partner stops me from seeing our kids?

Can my partner move away with the kids without my consent?

When it comes to our child's future care arrangements, what do I need to consider or put in place now?

Who are we required to tell that we've separated?

Is there a gender bias towards women in our family law legal system?

IMPORTANT TIME LIMITS

1
GETTING THE LAY OF THE LAND

INTRODUCTION

Knowing what needs to be sorted out from a legal and practical perspective after your split can be overwhelming.

Not all these matters will necessarily be relevant to you, so you can skip ahead as needed. Just remember, they are all separate matters from one another and need to be dealt with. For example, just because you agree on parenting, doesn't mean you've also sorted child support or vice versa.

1 WHAT NEEDS TO GET SORTED

Finances

After separating, couples generally need to work out a financial split: who is going to keep and be liable for what. This is formally known as a property settlement, which involves the division of assets, debts, and superannuation.

For some couples who don't have much to split or anything owned or owed jointly, they might decide that it's appropriate for them to each keep their own stuff. Even if a couple agrees to keeping their own stuff, there are reasons why it'd be in their interest to make that agreement official.

If you and your partner married, the law says you're automatically entitled to a financial split. This is separate from working out what is an appropriate division of the finances.

If you and your partner didn't marry, then for there to be a financial split, you must satisfy one of these requirements:

1. The total period of your de facto relationship must've been at least two years.

2. You and your partner must have a child (or children) together.

3. One of you must've made a substantial contribution and if a financial split didn't occur, there'd be a serious injustice.

4. You registered your de facto relationship under an Australian state or territory law.

Working out what is an appropriate financial split is explained in more detail in Chapter 5 (pages 125–150).

Parenting & child support

If you have a child or kids with your partner, then parenting (child custody) and child support are relevant and will need to be sorted. These two topics may still be relevant to you even if you don't share biological kids together. Parenting will cover anything to do with your child's care, welfare, and development. On the other hand, child support will deal with the financial support required to provide for your child or kids.

For more detail about parenting, see Chapter 3 (pages 79–104) and for more information about child support, read Chapter 4 (pages 105–124).

Maintenance (alimony)

Maintenance may be relevant to you in any of the following instances:

1. There's a big difference in your and your partner's individual incomes.

2. You or your partner are continuing to study or pursue qualifications.

3. Because of disability or health reasons, you or your partner don't work.

4. One of you is a stay-at-home parent.

Adult child maintenance

Adult child maintenance could be relevant if you have a child aged 17 or over, where financial support is necessary to enable he/she/them to complete their education and/or because of a mental or physical disability.

Divorce

Divorce is relevant if you and your partner married. You can't apply for divorce until after you've been separated for more than 12 months and one day.

Guy Advice

If you're going through a separation, I think my number one advice is, "Don't fight." It's never gonna turn out well... Obviously, it's fallen apart, so you're separating. Now you need to make practical decisions to make that separation work, which involve children, finances – they're the big ones. Children and finances. Those are the only two things that you really have to worry about because you cannot emotionally be there for that person anymore. I've never been able to emotionally be there for someone who I've separated or divorced from because you're not there anymore. That's been done away with, the emotional side of it, so it does become a very practical state of mind. You still give a hug and a kiss on the cheek, but you now need to keep the communication lines open and listen.

INTERIM ARRANGEMENTS

There needs to be a resolution on the topics identified above that are relevant to you. That's the direction you and your partner need to be heading – ideally, towards an agreement (versus an outcome imposed on you). Once you have an agreement, you can decide on whether you make that agreement official and if so, which way. I go into this in more detail on pages 192–199 of Chapter 9..

Now, until you and your partner have the agreement final, you'll probably need an interim arrangement in place. An interim arrangement is a holding pattern relating to what's to happen pending a final agreement and its implementation.

The below are answers to some FAQs that should prove handy.

Finances

Should one of us move out of the family home?

There can be reasons why you or your partner may want to consider moving out of the family home even though you don't have a financial separation agreement. Considerations for moving out might be:

- There's a lot of conflict between you and your partner.

- Your child or kids are being exposed to conflict between you and your partner.

- Your/your partner's mental health and physical wellbeing are deteriorating.

- You/your partner can afford it.

- For safety reasons.

Sometimes, however, it can be strategically better to remain living in the family home when you don't have a financial separation agreement. Considerations for remaining living in the family home might be:

- The uncomfortableness and pressure of living together can motivate you and your partner to reach a financial separation agreement together sooner rather than later (I've seen people take their foot off the brake when moving forward with the formal aspects of their separation once they and their partner start living apart. People get comfortable with the new living arrangements, so they're not necessarily incentivised to introduce further change or more uncertainty just yet, which formalising the separation would inevitably bring about).

- You/your partner can't afford to move out.

- You don't yet have a parenting agreement, and you're seeing the kids more than you would if you/your partner moved out.

- You/your partner prefer to immediately buy than rent/move out.

- Greater stability for your child or kids in remaining under the one roof.

Advice from an experienced family lawyer specific to you regarding whether you *should* move out will give you a complete answer to this question.

Does anyone have to move out of the family home?

No, unless there are sole occupation or family violence orders in place dealing with who can live in/go to the family home.

Can I change the locks to the home after my partner moves out?

Legally, yes – if house is registered in your sole name.
    Legally, yes – if house is registered in joint names.

If the house is registered in joint names, then your partner is legally entitled to change the locks again. You can also change them again though.

Can my partner change the locks to the house after I move out?

Legally, yes – if house is registered in her sole name.
Legally, yes – if house is registered in joint names.
If the house is registered in your partner's name, then you can't legally change the locks.
If the house is registered in your name or joint names, then you are entitled to legally change the locks. However, if you're no longer living in the family home, changing the locks mightn't be the best idea. This could be detrimental to your relationship, potentially being seen as intimidating, controlling, and harassing.
If you move out of the home altogether and you're considering changing the locks, reflect on the reasons why you're wanting to change them and get legal advice on this before doing anything.

How do I know if we're separated?

You'll know if you're separated because your relationship as a romantically-involved couple has been "brought to an end by the action or conduct of one only of the parties."[7] If your partner tells you she wants to separate or your partner decides that you are separating, that's also a telltale sign that you are separated.

Can we be separated but living under the same roof?

Yes.

Until we agree on a financial split, should we keep or change how we manage our finances and expenses?

It's a matter for you. Only legal advice specific to you would be able to answer this question and what's in your best interests and best for your family.

Some considerations for not changing your current financial arrangements might include:

- You're continuing to live together separated in the family home, and it makes sense to keep the financial arrangements in place until a financial split is agreed.

- You're the primary or only income earner and your partner relies on your income for financial support.

- You're not paying child support

- You're close to or anticipating reaching a financial separation agreement shortly.

Some considerations for changing your current financial arrangements might include:

- You've started paying child support to your partner.

- You're no longer living under the same roof.

- Your partner has changed the financial arrangements.

- Your partner refuses to contribute to the family and household expenses and has the capacity to.

- You've begun to separate your finances and expenses.

Maintenance may very well be relevant to you or your partner; in which case, how finances and expenses are managed will be important.

Do I have to pay the home loan if I'm no longer living there?

If the home loan is in your name or joint names, then you have a contractual obligation with your lender to pay the home loan. From your lender's perspective, if your name is anywhere on the home loan, you're 100 percent liable for it, even if it's in joint names. There can be implications on your credit history if the home loan is defaulted on.

The law says that after separating, each person is responsible for their own living expenses unless someone can't adequately support themselves. The inadequate support means there is a shortfall between a person's income and their individual expenses. This is where maintenance becomes relevant.

So, depending on what your income and individual expenses are, if there is a buffer (an excess), it may be appropriate, or a judge could require you, to pay or contribute to the home loan repayments even if you're not living there.

Does my partner have to contribute to the home loan even though she's not living there?

Like the answer above, if your partner's name is anywhere on the home loan, then she has a contractual obligation with the lender to pay the home loan.

Your and your partner's individual incomes and expenses are relevant to working out whether it's appropriate for your partner to contribute to or pay the home loan, that is, maintenance.

It's important that you're aware now that if you're looking to keep the home and take over the home loan, then payment of the home loan will impact the available house equity and, therefore, what's available to be divided between you and your partner.

To put this into context, if your partner starts paying rent elsewhere and doesn't contribute to the home loan and you're paying the loan, then you're reducing debt, which then increases what's available to be split between you.

The cost of your partner's rent isn't reducing debt or increasing what's available to be divided between you.

Note that just because you might be increasing the equity in the home, doesn't necessarily justify or equate to you receiving more of the pie. People can make after separation direct and indirect contributions. We go into more detail about this in Chapter 5 (pages 125–150).

Do I have to contribute to rent for the family home if I'm no longer living there?

If your name is on the lease for the family home, then you have a contractual obligation under your real estate agreement to pay the rent.

Whether you must contribute to rent for the family home from a family law perspective depends on your and your partner's individual incomes and expenses.

If you move out of the family home and start paying rent elsewhere, it could mean that you're unable to contribute to rent for the family home because you simply don't have the capacity to pay.

What steps should I consider taking now to protect me/us financially until we agree on a financial split?

- Freezing some or all joint bank accounts and credit cards, thereby preventing yourself and your partner from accessing these facilities

- Freezing the home loan repayments (noting that the bank may require you to make up the unpaid home loan repayments once the freeze period lifts)

- Cancelling secondary cardholders

- Putting a requirement for joint signatories on withdrawals from any home loan, line of credit, redraw facility, and joint bank accounts (whether that be altogether or for over a specific amount)

- Make a photocopy or email copies of financial documents to yourself

- Take photos of household contents, artwork, tools and equipment, memorabilia, and take screenshots of bank account balances and credit cards

- Tell your accountant, real estate agent, or financial advisor/planner

You need to be extremely careful in taking some of the above steps, more specifically, those actions that could or would cut off your partner's access to finances. Read the below question and answer.

Should I tell my partner about these protective interim financial steps?

It's a judgment call, and you need to be extremely careful in ensuring that you're making the right decision for your circumstances. Please read these next paragraphs very carefully.

Lies – lies by omission and perceived deceptive behaviours are hallmarks of a separation on the brink of turning nasty or involving lawyers. Why? Because they breed distrust.

If you tell your partner that you intend to take or have taken these protective interim steps, you risk your partner feeling disempowered, vulnerable, threatened, upset and fearful of what you'll do next. Your partner may feel dictated to and like you're calling all the shots. From your partner's perspective, this will very much be the case if you were the one who decided to end the relationship.

For women earning less than men or who feel they carry the greater parenting responsibility, some may be fearful of having no access to money, being cut off financially, and left unsupported while still being responsible for the kids' costs.

Regardless of whether you'd ever do this to your partner or not, your actions and her fears may prompt her to engage a lawyer. Understand that these potential fears are valid because we're talking about someone's feelings here.

On the other hand, sharing these interim protective steps with your partner can be a conversation starter, a collaborative decision to be made jointly.

For example, you could say, "Hey, I was thinking, given things are up in the air a bit with our finances, would you be against putting in place some freezes on our joint accounts and home loan so neither of us can access money over a certain amount without the other person's okay?"

When considering whether to tell your partner about these interim steps or deciding whether to do them at all, weigh the options against the risk of her taking the same steps, potentially freezing accounts or withdrawing money and then requesting a freeze.

You should be aware that taking some of the above interim financial steps can be considered financial abuse, which falls within the definition of family violence.

On this specific topic, you might want to get legal advice first because the actions taken can greatly influence what happens next. For example, if you cut off your partner's access to finances, then your partner could start court proceedings.

Child support

Do I have to pay child support if we're separated but living under the same roof?

It depends on whether you have a child support assessment and an agreed collection method.

If a child support assessment is in place and you're assessed as the parent required to pay, then legally you must pay the child support amount.

You can either have this paid through the child support collect option or as a private collect, which involves you and your partner agreeing on how and when payments will be made. You manage the payments between yourselves.

Some parents agree to the child support amount not being paid to the other parent if the person required to pay child support pays other expenses instead. See below for the differences between the three collect options.

Child support can be collected three different ways:

- **Self-management** – you and your partner agree on a child support amount, how and when it will be paid and manage the payments between you. No assessment is required, which means child support can't be backdated. This collection option means that you/your partner can't claim anything more than the base rate for Family Tax Benefit Part A.

- **Private collect** – you have a child support assessment but agree how and when payments will be made and managed between you. The Child Support Agency can only chase overdue child support payments going back up to three months in normal circumstances or up to nine months in exceptional circumstances.

- **Child Support collect** – you have a child support assessment in place, but the Child Support Agency manages the payment. The agency collects the child support amount from the parent required to pay and pays it to the other parent.

When do we need to apply for a child support assessment?

If you're not receiving any Centrelink benefits, there's no legal requirement to apply for a child support assessment.

If you're receiving a Centrelink benefit, you have an obligation to tell Centrelink about any change in circumstances, such as a change to your relationship.

Does it matter who applies for a child support assessment?

No, the parent who applies for the child support assessment isn't looked on more favourably than the parent who didn't apply.

Do we have to apply for a child support assessment?

Services Australia encourages parents to apply for a child support assessment if they receive the Family Tax Benefit Part A.

Family Tax Benefit Part A is a payment from the government for a dependent child who is either 0–15 years or 16–19 years old and studying. To be eligible for this benefit, there are a few other requirements, for example – and noting this list isn't exhaustive – an income test, residence, and a parent having at least 35 percent care of the child.

The assessed amount of child support payable to a parent impacts the amount of Family Tax Benefit Part A payable to that parent entitled to receive the child support. If that parent doesn't apply for a child support assessment and they receive the Family Tax Benefit Part A, they may only get the base rate of the benefit for the child.

If I or my partner receive maintenance or formal child support, do we have to tell Centrelink?

If you receive any Centrelink payments, then yes.

You have what's called a "maintenance income free area," which is an amount that you're allowed to receive without your Family Tax Benefit payment amount being impacted.

1 Parenting

Do we need to do anything formal about our child's care?

There's no legal requirement to do anything formal about your child's care. However, it is worth considering whether it's in your interests to have an interim written agreement, for example, a parenting plan, about your child's living and care arrangements. Read more about parenting plans on page 192 of Chapter 9.

Can my partner stop me from seeing our kids?

Practically speaking, yes.

There can be consequences for doing so though. Obvious consequences include your partner breaking your trust in her and, if your partner stops you seeing the kids for a prolonged period, having to figure out how your time with them should be reintroduced and managed. Your relationship with your children might also be damaged as a consequence.

If your partner unreasonably stops you from seeing the kids, I encourage you to get some legal advice from a family lawyer on what to do, and get it sooner rather than later. Doing nothing or delaying can work against you.

Can I stop my partner from seeing our kids?

Practically speaking, yes.

There are consequences for doing so though. Obvious ones include broken trust, resistance, or refusal by your partner to facilitate time between you and the kids, fearing that you mightn't return them.

If you believe stopping your partner from seeing your kids is necessary to protect their safety and wellbeing, you should certainly get legal advice, and do this as soon as possible.

What should I do if my partner stops me from seeing our kids?

- Write down what happened

- Keep a copy of the communications (texts and emails) to and from your partner

- Get some advice from an experience family lawyer – and quickly

Can my partner move away with the kids without my consent?

In the absence of court orders, practically speaking, yes. However, you can apply for a court order requiring your partner to return the children to the home state they left. You need legal advice on this, and you need to act quickly – as soon as you become aware of the possibility of your partner relocating with the children or it happening. If you don't act quickly and your partner moves away, you could be seen to have acquiesced to the move (basically consenting to the move), thereby possibly making it more difficult to have the children returned to their home state immediately.

If your partner wants to relocate interstate with the kids on a final basis and you don't agree, a judge will need to decide on whether that's in the kids' best interests.

1

When it comes to our child's future care arrangements, what do I need to consider or put in place now?

Advice from a lawyer will provide you with a specific answer on what to consider or put in place now. In the meantime, here are some considerations:

- Exercise caution when signing documents regarding your child. Signing documents, such as school enrolment forms, parenting plans, overseas travel, and passport applications, could have implications later when it comes to your child's care arrangements, child support and other matters. Consider getting advice beforehand so you understand the potential consequences.

- The regularity and duration of time that you spend with your child or kids now. If you spend just a few hours with your kids on a sporadic basis and go without seeing them for a week or more, with no real regularity, then you may struggle to press for immediate block periods of time with them. If a block period is appropriate, noting your kids' ages and unless you and your partner agree otherwise, a gradual increase in the kids' time with you may be more suitable longer term. When I say suitable, I say this from a child psychology developmental perspective.

- Your child's interim care and living arrangements. Interim arrangements generally impact your child's future care and living arrangements in the sense that rather than introducing a significant amount of change regarding their care arrangements, you gradually introduce it. This child-focused approach means you can properly support your child during the transition and avoid creating separation anxiety and attachment problems.

- Your child's or kids' ages. Children's developmental needs are greater the younger they are. Little ones, depending on your and your partner's involvement in caring for them on a day-to-day basis, mightn't cope with spending more than a few hours away from their primary attachment. If there isn't one right now, then a primary attachment may need to be established. What this means is that it might be more appropriate for your child to spend more time with one parent initially so that he or she can develop and maintain a sense of security.

- If you repeatedly cancel or fail to show up at time that you've agreed to have the kids. This can impact not only your partner's willingness to agree to an arrangement where you have your child or the kids more, but also the kids' relationship with you.

  And the same goes for your partner too. Years ago, I worked with a dad to four terrific kids – two boys, two girls. Mum ended the relationship, left the kids in Dad's care, and moved interstate. When this couple separated, their youngest child was six and their oldest was twelve. Dad repeatedly agreed to and facilitated time between Mum and the kids. The problem was that Mum repeatedly cancelled at short notice, didn't show altogether or left early. The kids were so disheartened, upset and beyond hurt.

  It put Dad in a difficult position because he needed to support and encourage the relationship between the kids and their mother. However, he could see the damage the children's mum was doing to their self-esteem and the relationship. The encouragement Dad gave to the kids came to negatively impact his relationship with them, so he stopped offering excuses for why Mum cancelled or didn't show up.

Consider keeping a diary of the dates, times, and durations that the kids are in your care and what you got up to. It need only be brief but if your partner suddenly stops facilitating time, you've got a contemporaneous record of your time with the kids. This can be very useful evidence when trying to reach a parenting agreement or, if you can't agree, then at court.

Other

Who are we required to tell that we've separated?

- **Centrelink** – if you're receiving any payments

- **Home Affairs** – if you're on a visa or sponsoring your partner's visa

- **Housing Department** – if you're living in public housing

- **Your employer** – if you require a security clearance or have an obligation as part of your employment/pay conditions to disclose any change in circumstances

- **Police** – if your relationship status is relevant to any criminal charges or bail conditions

You don't need to tell the court you're separated or lodge any documents.

Is there a gender bias towards women in our family law legal system?

In my opinion, there isn't a bias towards women or men written into our legislation. However, from my own personal observations at court, I do believe that gender stereotypes can potentially play a role.

For example, I worked with a dad who was the primary carer of four children. The mum started court proceedings for parenting and financial matters. Shortly after separating, the mum moved interstate and repartnered. When she returned to Canberra, she spent little time with the children, cancelled at short notice and returned the kids to the dad early. It seemed important to the judge that we explain the circumstances surrounding this couple's separation and the significant role that the dad played in the children's care throughout the relationship.

Another example, I worked with a young dad who had a little three-year-old boy. Dad was a fly-in fly-out worker who'd spend sporadic overnight time with his son when he returned to his home state for two consecutive nights at a time. When Dad returned to live full-time in his home state, Mum refused to facilitate overnight time. I prepared an affidavit that detailed Dad's involvement in his son's life and care, and how his proposed care arrangements would benefit his son. The details included what this dad had taught his son (for example, how to tie his shoes, ride a bike) and the other practical life lessons he would be able to teach and share if their son could spend more time with him. The female judge was greatly persuaded by this and ordered that Dad have his overnights with his son reinstated to three nights per fortnight, as well as day time contact, with his time to increase to four nights per fortnight within five months.

It's important to understand and appreciate that many of the couples who end up in court disputing a child's care arrangements have high needs and complex issues that must be dealt with. For example, mental health issues, a history of family violence, allegations of family violence and/or concerns for a child's safety. Unfortunately, the court system can be a means for a person to further abuse the other and for people to inflict irreparable damage on one another and their children.

A report conducted by the Australian Institute of Family Studies (October 2019) identified the following:

- Overall, in judge-made orders, parenting consent orders and private parenting agreements, it is most common for kids to spend the majority of their time with their mum and see their dad regularly.

- Where a parenting dispute went to trial and a judge made a decision, 11 percent of dads were allocated sole parental responsibility; 45 percent of mums were allocated sole parental responsibility, and equal shared parental responsibility was ordered in 44 percent of cases.[8]

IMPORTANT TIME LIMITS

Time limits – de facto couples

De facto couples have two years from the date they separate to:

- Reach a financial separation agreement and make it official

- If they don't have an official financial separation agreement, apply to the court to ask a judge to decide for them

- If it's relevant to them, reach a maintenance separation agreement and make it official

- If it's relevant to them and they don't have an official maintenance agreement, apply to the court for maintenance orders

If you and your partner are a de facto couple and you don't have a separation agreement within the two years after you separate, then everything remains as per legal title. This means that anything that is in your sole name is yours, and the same goes for your partner.

But – and this is a big but to be aware of – you and your partner could start court proceedings after the two-year limit expires and ask for a financial split. The person starting court proceedings would have to satisfy the judge that they'll suffer hardship if there isn't a financial split. This means that anything you own, inherit, accrue, save, or win is potentially up for grabs by your partner and vice versa. This also includes debts.

The same time limit applies to maintenance as well. If

you don't have an official resolution about maintenance, then you and your partner have two years from the date of your final separation to either reach an agreement – and make it official – or apply to the court for a judge to decide whether maintenance should be paid.

Time limits – married couples

For married couples, there are no time limits when it comes to financial and maintenance matters.

Time limits – divorced couples

For divorced couples, they have 12 months from the date of their divorce to:

- Reach a financial separation agreement and make it official

- If they don't have an official financial separation agreement, apply to the court and ask a judge to decide for them

- If it's relevant to them, reach a maintenance separation agreement and make it official

- If it's relevant to them and they don't have an official maintenance agreement, apply to the court for maintenance orders

If you and your partner were married, then divorced and don't have a separation agreement within the 12 months after your divorce, everything remains as per legal title. This means that anything that is in your sole name is yours, and the same goes for your partner.

But – this is important to understand – you and your partner could start court proceedings after the 12-month time limit expires and ask for a financial split. The person starting court proceedings would have to satisfy the judge that they'll suffer hardship if there isn't a financial split. This means that anything you own, inherit, accrue, save, or win, is potentially up for grabs by your partner and vice versa. This also includes debts.

The same time limit applies to maintenance as well. If you don't have an official resolution about maintenance before you divorce, then you and your partner have 12 months from the date of the divorce order to either reach an agreement – and make it official – or apply to the court for a judge to decide whether maintenance should be paid.

Time limits – couples who are parents

For parenting matters, there are no time limits. Parents can reach an agreement and decide to make it official at any point in time. If there's no agreement and a parent wants court orders dealing with their child's care, then they can apply to the court for parenting court orders at any point in time.

CHAPTER 2

Looking after You

2 LOOKING AFTER YOU

GRIEF CYCLE

ALARMING STATS & FACTS

BAD HEALTH CONTRIBUTORS
What coping strategies are there?

MANAGING THE RELATIONSHIP WITH YOUR PARTNER

GRIEF CYCLE

Like with death, there is a cycle of grief that you and your partner will likely experience in the lead up to or after the decision to separate.[9] There are five stages (depicted below), and you can expect to experience all five. The same goes for your partner.

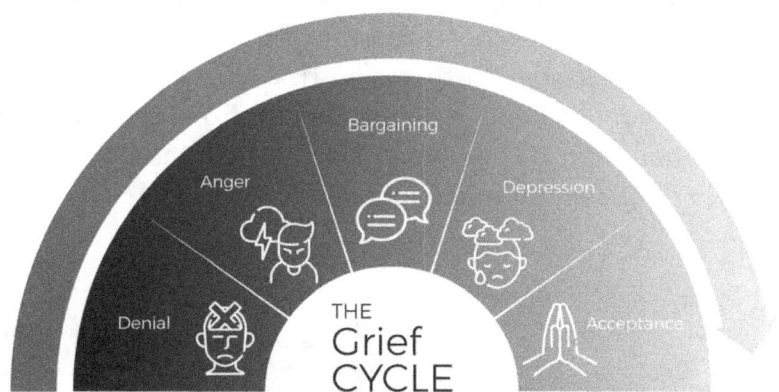

Many of the men who I've worked with have expressed feeling "blindsided" and "shocked" at their partner's decision to want to separate. This can be put down to either the partner checking out of the relationship and stopping communication or, from her perspective, the male not reading the signs, understanding what is being communicated by their partner or simply not listening.

- If your partner initiated the separation, then you can expect she'll be ahead of you in the grief cycle, having processed some of the early emotional grief cycle stages.

- If you initiated the separation, then you'll probably be ahead of your partner in the grief cycle. Women who I've worked with have also described feeling blindsided and shocked by their partner's decision to want to separate, but they also describe how he "checked out" months ago.

Just because someone has initiated the separation doesn't mean that they're fully over their grief for the relationship.

The thing is, to progress the practical aspects of finalising your separation in a formal way, you and your partner can't push one another ahead in the grief cycle before being ready. If you do that, you risk creating resistance, distrust, conflict, and disengagement from the process altogether from the person who is still in the very early stages of grieving the relationship.

Guy Advice

I guess my first bit of advice would be, are you 100 percent serious on it? Like, is it what you want? And then I would say, don't just do it because you think it's the right thing to do or you think it's the flavour of the month. Like, give it some thought. Even if you've got to split for a couple of months to move out or something, continue to talk if you can. But really give it some thought because, potentially, you'll regret it. And then I guess if it is what you decide – "No, I'm done" – I reckon, yeah, do what we did and come up with an agreement together because I know a lot of people that have spent a lot of money and 12 months later, they're still fighting. But I don't know, I guess everyone's different, too.

Why people separate

We've had close to a thousand people do our AMICABLE Separation Quiz, which is an online quiz that provides people with a personalised roadmap of suggested next steps to constructively move forward in their separation. The steps differ depending on which stage you're at: if you're thinking about separating, already separated, or separated with an agreement.

We ask people to identify the reasons why they're separating or thinking about it. Below are the top reasons in order of most common:

1. There is little or no intimacy, affection, or love.

2. My partner and I have simply grown apart.

3. We're not able to satisfy one another's wants or needs.

4. We've stopped communicating.

5. The relationship doesn't bring out the best in me.

6. My partner and I want different things out of life.

7. I've discovered that my partner and I have fundamentally different core life values.

8. I've simply fallen out of love with my partner.

9. I feel that my partner has stopped caring for and about me.

10. I'm unhappy in life generally, and I believe that ending the relationship is the right decision.

11. I feel ignored by my partner.

12. There has been infidelity (emotional and/or physical) by me, my partner or both of us.

13. I don't feel emotionally or physically safe with my partner.

14. I am/my partner is in love with someone else.

15. I fell into this relationship due to circumstances rather than my want and choice to be in it.

Getting some clarity as to the specific reasons why you believe you're separating – from your perspective and your partner's – can be helpful.

You can take The AMICABLE Separation Quiz.
Scan the below QR code.

ALARMING STATS & FACTS

Imagine this. The Melbourne Cricket Ground, filled to its capacity with 100,000 males. Of the 100,000 males seated, 18 will deliberately commit suicide over the next 12 months. About five of those men will be aged between 40–54 years.

Confronting, isn't it? You need to know about mental health because you, being male, have a much greater suicide rate than your female counterpart.

One of life's most challenging decisions is to separate. The upheaval, the emotional turmoil and vulnerability that this causes makes it all the more important for you to be prioritising your mental health and wellbeing.

We're talking for men:

- **18.6 deaths** per 100,000 people versus 5.8 deaths for women

- **43.6 years median** suicide age versus 43.1 years for women

- **75% of all suicides** each year versus 25% for women

- A study conducted in the UK in 2020 focusing on men's mental health after relationship breakdown found that child access and family court issues were the biggest contributors to low mental health and chronic stress among the separated male sample group.[10]

- Suicide is linked to depression and in 2020, there were 2,384 males in Australia who died by suicide. The median age was 43.6 years.[11] In 2020, the median age for men at the time of separating was 41.7 years.[12]

Guy Advice

After we separated, I initially struggled a lot. Like, I got really bad anxiety and if I would drink coffee or a pre-workout, my body would start shaking, and I couldn't think or concentrate. I was just anxious. So, I had to go to counselling, and that helped a lot, just to open up and talk to somebody that... Look, I spoke to them about anything. It sometimes didn't even relate to what was going on, but it was good having that person just to talk to and get it all out. I struggled with that for a little while, actually, just feeling anxious and nervous. And I don't know, I just couldn't shake it. These days it's good. Like, I haven't had it again. I think it was just all the stress and all the realization, and a few things happened. And yeah, it was really hard.

There's no doubt about it: chronic stress impacts your health in ways you're probably unaware of.

LOOKING AFTER YOU

Your cardiovascular system

An ongoing increased heart rate, higher stress hormone levels and blood pressure can lead to a heart attack, stroke and hypertension.

Your musculoskeletal system

Muscle tension can lead to physical injuries in day-to-day activities and cause headaches and migraines.

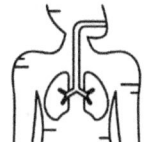

Your respiratory system

Ever had shortness of breath or breathed rapidly? Chronic stress causes your body to breathe this way, restricting the airway between your nose and lungs. Existing respiratory conditions, like asthma, can be further exacerbated.

Your gut system

Chronic stress impacts your gut bacteria. Think spasming bowel muscles, bloating, weakened intestinal barrier, increased or decreased appetite, heartburn, and impact on your mood and your ability to think and process emotions.

Your nervous system

Being in a constant stage of fight-or-flight due to chronic stress can lead to wear and tear on your nervous system, which becomes problematic to the other areas in your body that work with that system.

Your reproductive system

Stress can see an increase in the release of cortisol, which impacts your libido, sperm production and maturation, and can compromise male anatomy leading to infection.[13]

ALARMING STATS & FACTS

BAD HEALTH CONTRIBUTORS

There are actions you can take now upstream that can minimise the risk of you experiencing reduced mental health and wellbeing.

Get ahead of yourself now and take a moment to reflect on what could lead you to feel, or be in a position of, reduced mental health and wellbeing.

- If you predominantly socialised with your partner's friends or family, or they were your support system, then you may find that that system or friendship falls away. This can contribute to feelings of loneliness.

- Work stress.

- Not seeing your children or having certainty about when you will.

- Emotions associated with processing the end of the relationship.

All those outdated sayings of "man up," "take it on the chin" and "just get on with it" don't apply. In fact, they never applied. Let's get real then about what practical coping strategies are out there.

What coping strategies are there?

Looking after your mental health has never been more important than now.

You're deserving of help, and it's out there if you choose to get it. Coping strategies include:

- One-on-one counselling

- Phone counselling

- Support groups

- Online self-paced courses that focus on your self-esteem, mental health, and coping strategies

- Friends

Men do re-partner quicker than women after separating. Be mindful that if you're entertaining a new relationship or moving forward, this might be a reactive or unconscious decision by you, with the new relationship being a coping strategy to look after yourself by feeling that someone else cares for you.

Guy Advice

Get help. I think your emotional state is more important than your financial state. You need to make sure you're going to be emotionally stable because you're no use to anybody if you're not.

2

LOOKING AFTER YOU

If you have any of these behaviours or signs, jump on it and get in touch with either your general practitioner (GP) or a male support focused organisation (details below):

Loneliness	Distress	Panic/panic attacks
Feelings of worthlessness	Thoughts of self-harm	Suicidal thoughts
Difficulty sleeping	Self-harm	Difficulty concentrating
Overwhelm	Feelings of dread	Negative thoughts
Sadness	Loss of appetite	Inability to laugh
Increased alcohol consumption	Using/increased use of illicit substances	Disinterest in activities, friends & hobbies
Anxiety	Sobbing/crying	Lower energy levels
Chest pains	Gut discomfort – bloating, nausea, pain, bowel muscle spasms	

Guy Advice

I think that's my best advice: do not self-destruct yourself. Make sure you get help, make sure you've got good friends around you, make sure you talk to someone, whether it's a friend or a counsellor. And, as I say, go through the counsellors and find someone who you can talk to.

Please note that this is a resource list only – it is not an endorsement for the service/organisation itself. Please make your own enquiries and exercise good judgment in deciding what's right for you.

Counselling services:

- MensLine Australia – www.mensline.org.au

- Black Dog Institute – www.blackdoginstitute.org.au

- 1800Respect – www.1800respect.org.au

- Beyond Blue – www.beyondblue.org.au/who-does-it-affect/men

- Blokes Psychology – www.blokespsychology.com.au

This next part perhaps doesn't need to be stated, but I'll state it all the same. Sure, it might come across as a bit superficial, but there's science behind it all.

To make things that little bit easier, you can get this list as a downloadable PDF from the interactive book at deanpublishing.com/siobhanmullins

Create structure
Separating from someone you share a life with can be emotionally tumultuous. You can feel out of control and filled with feelings of uncertainty.

Get yourself into a routine to create stability and structure. For example, Wednesdays is when you meet with a friend for a catch up; it's when you take a walk in the park before heading home after work, or it's when you do your household chores.

Sleep
Go to bed at a decent time. You should be getting conservatively six hours of sleep each night to function at minimum. Ideally, you want to be aiming for seven or more hours.

If you're waking in the middle of the night, a hops tea might do the trick. If you're waking in the middle of the night for a bathroom break, consider stopping drinking liquids at least two hours before bed so you can sleep through.

If you're struggling to fall and stay asleep, it's probably time for a visit to your GP to talk about this and see what they recommend.

Practice mindfulness

I haven't really delved into mindfulness (mediation) because I can be a fairly impatient person, and the thought of just sitting there breathing gives me anxiety. But there are so many benefits from practicing mindfulness.

I'm suggesting you do one simple thing – assuming you don't do it already. Check out the Balance App: www.balanceapp.com. As of 24 June 2022, the app is free to use for the first 12 months.

What have you to lose in giving it a go?

Exercise

Sweat produces the chemical androsterone, which is a pheromone produced in males by the adrenal gland and testes. Women also produce pheromones but at a reduced amount. For men, the pheromones produced are released through skin, hair, and urine.

Pheromones increase testosterone, reduce anxiety and depression, and otherwise are a mood booster, relaxer and good for improving confidence.

Guy Advice

The gym was a really good one for me. It was a stress relief. You could pump it out on the road, get on the rowing machine, or go for a four-k run on the treadmill. I found that really helpful. Extremely helpful. Yeah, exercise is a big thing for me.

Aside from the obvious benefits to your physical health and heart, exercise is good for your waistline too.

So, what will you do to increase your sweat to get your pheromones pumping?

Guy Advice

Yeah, I went to the gym every day. I was doing that, but it was just because I wanted to. But not really. I sort of... I don't know. I don't do a lot for myself. I've been doing a little bit for myself lately.

Eat right

Make a conscious and active choice to eat more fresh fruit and vegetables.

Eat it at smoko or if you don't generally have morning or afternoon tea, then introduce some fresh fruit into your diet elsewhere.

Drink right

Alcohol is a known depressant. It's a mood destabiliser although used a lot as a crutch to manage emotions. Make a judgment call about reducing, limiting, or eliminating alcohol altogether.

If you're a recreational and regular user of drugs, whether that be marijuana, cocaine, ecstasy or whatever else is the trend, be cautious and mindful about your usage.

IMPORTANT: If you have a child, know that abuse of prescription medications, use of illegal substances and excessive alcohol consumption will be extremely relevant to your child's care and living arrangements. The law is very clear that children need to be protected from harm and the risk of exposure. If you or your partner do use, even recreationally, you will want to seriously consider getting help to manage or stop altogether. Allegations of excessive alcohol consumption, abuse of prescription meds and illicit substances can see a parent's time with their child be supervised, reduced, or stopped altogether. If you have concerns for your child's safety in your partner's care because of these matters or even for mental health reasons, I strongly encourage you to get legal advice as soon as possible.

Set yourself a challenge of replacing one alcoholic drink with a herbal tea, kombucha or fresh juice.

Dress the part
Replace any daggy socks or briefs you've got. It's the small things that count in helping you feel more confident.

Get a haircut and trim any wild body hair that you're not enamoured with, whether it's nasal hair, ear hair, chest, shoulder, or neck hair.

Smell the part
Personal hygiene is important for yourself – and those around you! Remember the deodorant, daily showers and if you really want to step it up, put on daily cologne, even if you're going to the grocery shop or work.

Be discreet
When it comes to your romantic or sex life, be discreet. The same goes for your social media. Don't be posting anything about your separation or your partner, including anything that could be construed as you having a go at her.

I had a colleague who worked with a woman who had experienced physical violence from her husband. The husband "liked" and "shared" a post on his social media about the Brad Pitt and Angelina Jolie movie, *Mr & Mrs Smith*. Given the storyline and the husband's past violence, the wife felt threatened by the husband's social media activity in this instance. The wife applied for and was granted a Family Violence Order against the husband. You might read this as a ridiculous example and overreaction by the wife. The husband's action must be seen in the context of his past behaviours though. Our legal system takes a very protective stance for people who reasonably fear for their safety.

Be very careful and mindful of sharing photos of your kids online, including dating sites. Question whether you need to share photos and videos of your kids with all your social media friends.

I worked with a mum, who had two girls aged seven and twelve years. The dad had photos of him with the girls in their swimmers on his dating profile. Now aside from the girls being underage, not having had the opportunity to consent to a digital footprint being created on their behalf, they weren't fully clothed. When Mum learnt about the photos on Dad's profile, she was upset. Shoe on the other foot, if your partner featured photos of herself with the kids, consider how you'd feel with other males viewing those photos. You might be able to understand Mum's upset in this instance.

To let you know of the outcome, Dad refused to remove the photos, which only caused more angst between him and Mum.

MANAGING THE RELATIONSHIP WITH YOUR PARTNER

Trigger words and phrases to avoid

The reality is communication with your partner after you separate is likely to further deteriorate rather than improve. That is, unless you work on your communication.

Below is a list of trigger words and phrases that you can replace with constructive, neutral, and non-emotive words and responses.

Instead of...	Use this...	The Logic
Entitled	Allowed	"Entitled" is positional and defensive.
Fair	Appropriate	"Fair" is a subjective term and fairness has a different meaning to each person. It's inflammatory because generally if you're using the word "fair," you're implying that what you say is fair, thereby accusing the other person of being unfair.
But or however	Just don't use those words!	Using either of these words renders your previous statement redundant. Your partner focuses on your "but" statement, which will generally be argumentative and positional. They end up ignoring your previous statement altogether.
Why?	What makes this necessary? What makes that important to you?	"Why" makes people feel accused and interrogated. The alternative phrase aims to prompt your partner to think constructively about her reasons for what she has proposed should happen.
How will you be able ...	How can we ...	"We" versus "you" implies a collaborative teamwork effort, which is what you want in order to avoid your partner being on the backfoot and having to feel like she's against you and doing it alone.

LOOKING AFTER YOU

I propose/ suggest/ offer	**Would you be against ...**	People feel safer in saying "no." You want to elicit as many "no's" from your partner because a "yes" signifies commitment, and people are wary about committing themselves when feeling unsafe and vulnerable.
Get real/ as if/that's stupid	**How am I supposed to do that?/How do I overcome the challenges I have here?**	Tone is important to this phrase, which aims to prompt your partner to constructively think about *how* you might be able to execute what she has proposed.
You don't make any sense	**Help me to understand**	This phrase seeks to understand what your partner has said and doesn't accuse her of not making sense.
I'm not being unfair	**I'm happy to be shown how I'm being unfair**	This phrase seeks to understand your partner's thought process and why she thinks what you've said is unreasonable.
You're lying	**It seems like there's something bothering you/It seems like there's more to this than what you're saying**	This phrase is about recognising a difference in someone's behaviour, potentially because of a lie, without accusing them and causing them to become defensive.
I'm not lying	**Why would it be in my interests to lie to you?**	This phrase prompts your partner to reflect on the reasons she believes you're lying versus having you go on the backfoot and become defensive with her.
Don't get upset at me	**It seems like what I said upset you**	This phrase signals to your partner that you're reading the situation and are in touch with what's going on for her emotionally. It's a check in and, for you, comes from a place of seeking understanding. For your partner, she may see it as you caring.
Which idea/ proposal do you like/ want/agree with?	**Which idea/ proposal do you most prefer?**	Expressing a preference for an option means you're narrowing down what needs to be decided on without firmly committing to a specific outcome. It's collaborative and constructive, versus your partner saying, "I hate all your options/ideas" or "I don't agree to anything."

How to communicate (text, email, and conversation)

When it comes to how you and your partner can get in touch with one another, you've got email, and you've got your mobile phone for text messages, videos, voice messages and phone calls. You can positively leverage these different means of communication to establish boundaries and respect for each other.

Text message

Good for...	Not good for...	Logic
Urgent issues - the kids are sick, the house is on fire Handover - running late/you've arrived Courtesies - acknowledgments that you've received their email/text and you plan on responding in X days or, kids are sick keeping home from school	Separating emotions Getting breathing space from your partner Giving your partner breathing space Resolving conflict Boundary setting	Because we're contactable on our mobile phones 24/7, they can be a means of exerting control over the other person or feeling like you're being controlled. Communications are instantaneous, and there's an expectation of an immediate or fast response. Because of the immediacy of the contact, the receiver is confronted with the communication; he or she doesn't quite have the choice of learning of the communication in their own time. This can be suffocating, upsetting, and feel like a boundary violation. People are reactive to messages and calls received on their phone. Emotions more easily get in the way.

Tips for communicating via text message
- Keep it short, keep it simple.
- If you're asking more than two questions that are unrelated, send your partner an email instead.

- If it's that important that you receive a response from your partner sooner rather than later, then send your partner a text message saying something to the effect of, "Hey [name], I've just sent you an email re: [topic]. If you could please have a read when you get a chance and let me know as soon as you can? Thanks in advance."

Email Communications

Good for...	Not good for...	Logic
Formulating plans Presenting offers or proposals Exchanging information, such as documents, spreadsheets, financial disclosure Contacting third parties, such as real estate agents	Unleashing emotions, blame and accusations	People are more reflective of the emails they write. Writers are given the opportunity to prepare the email, save it in draft and send it later. The expectation of an immediate response isn't there, unlike with texting. The reader is given the opportunity to read the email, digest what they've read, sit on it and respond in their own time. Each person can log into their email when they want. They have control and autonomy. It means that if they're not in the right headspace to deal with a subject matter, they're not confronted with a situation where they must then deal with it.

Tips for communicating via email
- Remove the diatribe and emotion.
- Keep what you say high level, without any accusations.
- Don't argue or respond to every single point of your partner's email. You don't agree, do you need to explain why? How likely are you

to persuade your partner otherwise? What do you gain and lose by addressing every point? Sometimes it's better to say, "I don't think it's going to be helpful for us to go back and forth on this issue, so I won't respond to what you've said. I'll just focus on [abc]."

- Write your email and wait 24 hours before sending it to your partner. Re-read the email and make any changes that you feel are appropriate.
- Less is more. General rule of thumb when it comes to email is the less you say, the better. There's less to dispute or get emotional over.
- Consider getting a sensible person to read over your email and provide any comments or feedback they might have regarding what you've written.

Guy Advice

Emails worked better for me personally as a male because I forget what I've said, so an email is proof that I said something even though they can get a bit nasty sometimes. But you need to cut the emotional side of things away and get to the chase. I'm a dot point man, so this is how we need to address all these things, everything from pets to whatever, to make things work.

Conversations

Phone conversations mightn't be the best means of communicating with your partner about detailed matters.

The biggest reason is that you can't see your partner, which means you can't read the whole situation – her body language, facial expressions, and emotions.

How we communicate is broken down into:
- 7% what we say
- 38% in tone
- 55% body language[14]

By talking on the phone and removing visual cues, you're missing out on more than half of what your partner is outputting. If you're wondering whether Facetime (a video call) would help, it's an improvement on a phone call, but generally this is done on a mobile, where people aren't seated and concentrating.

Guy Advice

Get it in writing so there's no miscommunication. You said you'd do that, you didn't. If most guys are like me, I go, "Did I? I didn't say that. If I did say that, that's not what I meant." So we need to keep things on track, keep things to the point, don't get personal, don't attack the new boyfriend, don't make things worse than what they should be.

In terms of how you'd coordinate a face-to-face conversation with your partner, you'd start by suggesting it to them and outlining the purpose of the conversation. This signals that there is an agenda to keep you both on track with your conversation.

Good for...	Not good for...	Logic
Boundary setting Constructive, purposeful, and productive conversations designed to get momentum. You've got a plan of what will be discussed, with a preview of objectives and achieving next steps Reading your partner's emotions The ability to communicate visually with body language	Rehashing the relationship People who feel physically unsafe with their partner	If you met face-to-face for a conversation, you could do it over coffee, in which case the discussion would perhaps be limited to around 20 minutes unless you both agree to continue beyond then. You're both in public, so you've got to be on your best behaviour. If the conversation turns south or someone turns revolting, then a person can leave.

Tips for the face-to-face conversation
- You'll have communicated by email before, exchanging information or coming up with a plan about what needs to be discussed at the face-to-face meeting.
- Bring pen and paper with you so you can write anything important down, including the agreed outcomes.
- Agree ahead of time how long you'll meet for.
- Agree to meet in a public place – not at either of your homes. After a couple separate, a person's

home becomes their sanctuary, their private retreat and space. If you and your partner still live under the one roof, a conversation outside of the home's four walls creates space and boundaries. You're not chasing one another around the house trying to continue a conversation when someone wants it to stop. You're not springing conversations on one another at random times with no notice.

- Start the conversation with pleasantries and lead with what you're both likely to agree on, for example, "Thanks for agreeing to meet today. I think it's positive we're here meeting for about X minutes to talk about Y. I think we probably both agree it's going to be important for us to hear one another out, not talk over one another and not rehash our relationship. Are there any ground rules you want to set now before we make a start?"

I realise that certain conditions may make a face-to-face coffee difficult, so an alternative to this is setting up an online meeting with cameras on, for example, through Teams, Zoom or Skype. The same tips as above apply to conversations facilitated in an online meeting.

CHAPTER 3

Parenting

3 PARENTING

INTRODUCTION
WHAT THE LAW SAYS
EXAMPLES OF PARENTING AGREEMENTS
FAQS

Can she make decisions about the kids without my consent?

Do women always get primary care of the kids?

Can men get primary care of the kids?

Can we have a parenting agreement without involving lawyers?

Does our parenting agreement have to be approved by a judge?

When does what our kids want become relevant?

How long do we lock in our child's care and living arrangements for?

Can she move away with the kids without my consent?

Do we have to let the Child Support Agency know about our parenting agreement?

What determines who gets custody of a child?

How do we decide on our child's care arrangements?

We've been equal carers to our child. How do we work out our child's care when we start living separately and apart?

Can we change our parenting agreement in the future if we both agree?

Can I get full-time sole care of our kids?

I was primary carer of our kids when my partner and I were together. Will I continue to be primary carer?

How does our child's care impact child support?

I have genuine concerns about our child's safety with my partner. What do I do?

When is a 50/50 care arrangement considered appropriate for a child?

My partner wants me to do a drug test before I see our child. Can she make me do this?

What should we consider including in our parenting agreement?

Does cheating impact child custody?

I don't have permanent housing now. Does that mean I can't have overnights with the kids?

PARENTING APPS

INTRODUCTION

You're a dad. You love your child or kids and want the best for them. When you got together with your child's mum, you probably didn't plan on separating. Now you're in a situation where you've got to work out how you and your partner can continue to parent, not inflict damage on your kids and still co-parent, all the while living in two separate homes.

How do you do that?

Know this. The law on parenting after separation is founded on child psychology principles and theories. Lawyers can tell you what the law says, how Judges are likely to apply it in your circumstances based on what you tell them – for example, your and your partner's involvement in your child's care when you were together, your child's age and the practicalities of a care arrangement – to then advise you what an appropriate care arrangement would like look.

That's all well and good, but you know as well as I do that your child's care arrangements must work practically. They've got to reconcile with your child's happiness and wellbeing, and that of your partner's and your own.

Shift worker? Construction worker? With your work hours, you mightn't be able to commit to set days and times for the year or have the kids during the school week without some extra help in the early mornings so you can get to work and they can get to school on time.

Plenty of parents across the country work out their kids' care around such work arrangements, reconciling with their child's needs. We go into how to work with your partner to reach a parenting agreement in Chapter 9 (pages 187–199).

3 WHAT THE LAW SAYS

The law about parenting after separation strives to ensure that kids have the benefit of meaningful involvement from their parents, are protected from harm, achieve their full potential and that parents fulfil their obligations in caring for their kids.

The law says that care arrangements for children after their parents separate should be those in their best interests.

What does "best interests" mean? Well, there are two primary considerations:

- The benefit of a child having a meaningful relationship with each parent

- The need to protect a child from harm

Other considerations include:

- Your child's views (subject to age, maturity, and level of understanding)

- Your child's relationship with you and your partner and any other relevant people, such as relatives

- The extent to which you or your partner have or haven't taken the opportunity to participate in long-term decisions about your child and spend time and communicate with them

- The extent to which you and your partner have fulfilled, or not, your financial support obligations to your child (that is, payment of child support and additional expenses)

- The likely effect of any changes to your child's circumstances, including being separated from each parent, other siblings, or other people who your child has been living with

- The practical difficulty and expense of your child spending time and communication with you and your partner and whether that will substantially affect your child's right to maintain a relationship and contact with you and your partner on a regular basis

- Your and your partner's capacity to provide for your child's needs – emotionally, intellectually, and financially

- Your child's, your, and your partner's characteristics, lifestyle, culture, sex and maturity

- If your child is Aboriginal or Torres Strait Islander, then their right to enjoy their culture and the impact that any proposed parenting order would have on that right

- Your and your partner's demonstrated attitudes to your child and your parenthood responsibilities

- Any family violence experienced by your child, you, your partner, or other family members

- If a family violence order applies or has applied, then various considerations regarding the order and supporting evidence

As you can see, what determines your child's care arrangements is an art not a science.

3 EXAMPLES OF PARENTING AGREEMENTS

Real-life parenting agreement 1:

- Two kids, three and seven years.

- Mum works part-time hours.

- Dad works full-time, standard hours.

- Dad has the kids six nights a fortnight, and Mum has them eight nights a fortnight.

	Week 1	Week 2
Mon-Tue	Mum	Mum
Tues-Wed	Mum	Mum
Wed-Thur	Dad	Dad
Thur-Fri	Dad	Dad
Fri-Sat	Dad	Mum
Sat-Sun	Dad	Mum
Sun-Mon	Mum	Mum

Real-life parenting agreement 2:

- One child aged two years.

- Mum works part-time hours.

- Dad works full-time but in construction with 6:00 am morning starts.

- Dad has their daughter three nights a fortnight, every Thursday afternoon and time on Sunday in Week 2 for at least half of the day.

- Parents agreed they'd look at increasing their daughter's time with Dad when she turns three.

	Week 1	Week 2
Mon-Tue	Mum	Mum
Tues-Wed	Dad	Dad
Wed-Thur	Mum	Mum
Thur-Fri	Dad (afternoon) Mum	Dad (afternoon) Mum
Fri-Sat	Mum	Mum
Sat-Sun	Dad	Mum
Sun-Mon	Mum	Dad (half the day) Mum

3 PARENTING

Real-life parenting agreement 3:

- One child aged ten years.

- Mum works full-time hours as a nurse – so shift work.

- Dad works full-time hours in construction – early morning starts.

- Mum and Dad have their son seven nights a fortnight (50/50), with handover happening each Friday after school.

	Week 1	Week 2
Mon-Tue	Mum	Dad
Tues-Wed	Mum	Dad
Wed-Thur	Mum	Dad
Thur-Fri	Mum	Dad
Fri-Sat	Dad	Mum
Sat-Sun	Dad	Mum
Sun-Mon	Dad	Mum

Real-life parenting agreement 4:

- Two children aged six and eight years. One has special needs.

- Mum works full-time hours.

- Dad works full-time hours – shift worker.

- Dad has the kids one overnight a fortnight and may have an extra night with their youngest in the fortnight. Dad otherwise has the kids three to four afternoons a week. Mum otherwise has the kids.

	Week 1	Week 2
Mon-Tue	Mum	Mum
Tues-Wed	Mum	Dad (afternoon) Mum
Wed-Thur	Dad	Dad (afternoon) Mum
Thur-Fri	Dad (afternoon) Mum	Dad (afternoon) Mum
Fri-Sat	Dad (afternoon) Mum	Dad (afternoon) Mum
Sat-Sun	Mum	Mum
Sun-Mon	Mum	Mum

Real-life parenting agreement 5:

- Two kids aged five and ten years.

- Mum works full-time standard hours.

- Dad works full-time standard hours.

- Dad has the kids five nights a fortnight, and Mum has the kids nine nights a fortnight. The kids know that regardless of the week, they'll spend each Thursday overnight with their dad.

	Week 1	Week 2
Mon-Tue	Mum	Mum
Tues-Wed	Mum	Mum
Wed-Thur	Mum	Mum
Thur-Fri	Dad	Dad
Fri-Sat	Dad	Mum
Sat-Sun	Dad	Mum
Sun-Mon	Dad	Mum

Note that in all of the above examples, there were no concerns from either parent regarding any substance or alcohol abuse or mental health issues.

General comments

Fortnightly arrangements are common because then the kids get a weekend with each parent.

Depending on a child's age, returning them on a Sunday afternoon/early evening to the parent they primarily live with can be good for preparing the child for the start of the school week, as it always starts the same.

Sometimes parents want to limit the number of times they have to meet (to hand over the kids). This might be because of fear of conflict with the other parent, worries for their safety or simply practical reasons. Parents then agree for the day that the kids change houses to be a school day, meaning the kids go directly to the other parent's home after school.

With example five, these parents may decide that when their youngest is a bit older they drop the Thursday overnight in Week 2 and make it a Wednesday overnight in Week 1. This would see the kids have one less change each fortnight and consolidate the nights the kids are with their dad into one block period of five nights.

Guy Advice

When this all first happened, I probably didn't have contact with the kids for three or four months, which, emotionally, was very difficult for me. I made a few mistakes there. I tried to explain to the girls what happened and what their mum did to me, and that was wrong. They're too young, and even if they were older, I don't think that's helpful because you just pin one parent against the other. I didn't want that to happen. They knew their mum loved them both, and they knew that I loved them and that we needed that time apart. I think having that three to four months of not much contact, the occasional text message, was good, just to let things calm down. And then I still remember three or four months later when I got the girls round for dinner. I got them round for dinner at my place and I was a nervous wreck.

FAQS

Can she make decisions about the kids without my consent?

It depends on the types of decisions and whether you have court orders in place about your child.

If your child is in your partner's care and becomes sick, then your partner could decide not to send your child to school. That's called day-to-day parental responsibility which, unless you have a court order saying otherwise, doesn't require your consent.

On the other hand, long-term decisions, such as your child's school, whether they receive a COVID vaccination, and if they have a broken arm whether it gets fixed, would require your consent unless there are court orders in place saying otherwise.

Do women always get primary care of the kids?

No.

Can men get primary care of the kids?

Yes, it is possible. This can either be agreed to by each parent or decided by a judge if the judge is satisfied that it's in a child's best interests for this to happen.

Can we have a parenting agreement without involving lawyers?

Yes. There's no legal requirement to involve lawyers to reach a parenting agreement.

Depending on whether you choose to make your parenting agreement official and which way, you may need help from a lawyer for the paperwork side of things. We go into all this in Chapter 9 (pages 187–199).

Does our parenting agreement have to be approved by a judge?

No. There's no legal requirement to make your parenting agreement official, let alone have it approved by a judge.

We dive into more detail about the different ways you can make your parenting agreement official on pages 192–193 of Chapter 9.

When does what our kids want become relevant?

Upwards of ten years, subject to maturity and their level of understanding.

A child's views don't dictate their care or living arrangements but can certainly be an influencing factor in what parents agree should happen or if parents can't agree, then what a judge decides.

How long do we lock in our child's care and living arrangements for?

It's really a matter for you and your partner to decide on. If you go to court and a judge must decide for you, the arrangements will be locked in until your child turns 18.

Depending on your child's age, you mightn't want to lock in arrangements until they're 18. For babies and young children, you might instead want to agree to an arrangement for three or six months with a review date. For school aged children, you might want to review this each year or every second year.

A review date allows you and your partner to:

- Reflect on how well the arrangements are working for you both and, importantly, your child

- Make changes to the arrangements, which might include increasing a parent's time with your child

- Introduce new changes to better support your child or deal with any issues

Can she move away with the kids without my consent?

If there are no parenting court orders in place dealing with parental responsibility, then practically speaking, yes.

However, you can apply for a parenting court order that requires your partner to return the kids to their home state. If a relocation by your partner with the children is a possibility or it happens, I encourage you to act quickly and get legal advice from an experienced family lawyer.

There can be implications if you do nothing or delay.

Do we have to let the Child Support Agency know about our parenting agreement?

If you apply for or have a child support assessment, then the Child Support Agency will need to know about your parenting agreement – more specifically the number of overnights your child is with each of you.

What determines who gets custody of a child?

What will be relevant and influence your child's care and living arrangements can include:

- Your child's ages

- Your and your partner's level of involvement in your child's care

- The regularity and duration of your and your partner's time with your child

- Any sibling relationships

- The distance between your and your partner's home and your child's school/day care

- Your and your partner's housing circumstances

- Your child's personality and developmental needs

- Your supportiveness for your child's relationship with their mum

- Your partner's supportiveness of your relationship with your child

For more information on the legal principles that guided judges in making decisions on who a child lives or spends time with, see the beginning of this chapter.

How do we decide on our child's care arrangements?

Start with what's already agreed and work backwards to identify what requires agreement.

For example, for their three children, Jack and Jill agree:

- They'll share joint parental responsibility.

- The kids will live primarily with Jill during the school term.

- The kids will spend half of the school holiday periods with Jack and Jill each.

- Once their youngest turns eight (in eight months' time), the kids will start living on a week about basis (50/50).

- The kids will spend time with each parent on special occasions, like birthdays.

Jack and Jill essentially then need to decide on:

- The number of overnights the kids are with Jack during the school term until their youngest turns eight years

- How to transition to the week about arrangement after their youngest turns eight so the kids are best supported

For more on the different ways you and your partner can work together to reach a parenting agreement, read pages 190–191 of Chapter 9.

We've been equal carers to our child. How do we work out our child's care when we start living separately and apart?

It's going to be a matter for you both to work together on to decide. Whether it's appropriate to immediately start a 50/50 arrangement will depend on your children's ages.

Read pages 190–191 of Chapter 9 to discover who can help you work through this together.

Can we change our parenting agreement in the future if we both agree?

Yes, in any of the following instances:

- If you don't make your parenting agreement official

- If your parenting agreement is in a parenting plan

- If your parenting agreement is in a parenting consent order

If you had parenting orders made by a judge after going to trial, then you mightn't be able to change the orders. However, you could potentially have the changes documented in a parenting plan, assuming the orders didn't exclude you from doing this. When it comes to changing parenting orders, you'd want to get advice from a lawyer.

Can I get full-time sole care of our kids?

Potentially, yes.

I was primary carer of our kids when my partner and I were together. Will I continue to be primary carer?

It all depends.

It depends on what you and your partner both agree on, or if you can't agree and a judge gets involved, then what the judge decides.

Consider all practicalities regarding how you're capable of continuing to primarily care for your child, from your work hours and commitments, your child's needs, the distance from home to your child's school/day care and the like.

How does our child's care impact child support?

The number of overnights that your child is in your and your partner's care impacts the child support amount that you or your partner could be required to pay.

I have genuine concerns about our child's safety with my partner. What do I do?

Get legal advice and do so as soon as possible.

When is a 50/50 care arrangement considered appropriate for a child?

In addition to the below considerations, a 50/50 care arrangement for your child has to be age appropriate. The expectation that a newborn, who might still be being breastfed, should live with each parent 50/50 is simply not appropriate. Such an arrangement won't be in that child's best interests.

Children who are introduced to a 50/50 care arrangement quickly and at a very young age can experience separation anxiety and attachment problems. These can become lifelong issues if not dealt with.

- Communication between parents is positive and constructive.

- Parents are supportive of their child's relationship with each parent.

- Parents appropriately satisfy their child's needs, for example, cultural, developmental, financial.

- A child has a healthy attachment to each parent.

Exploring when or if a 50/50 care arrangement for your child is appropriate is best explored with a child psychologist or mediation.

My partner wants me to do a drug test before I see our child. Can she make me do this?

Don't skip reading the full answer to this question!

If there are no parenting court orders in place requiring you to perform a drug test before you see your child, then your partner can't make you do anything.

One parent might insist on the other performing a drug test before facilitating time for any of the following reasons:

- They have concerns about, or there is a history of, illicit substance abuse. They might want peace of mind knowing that the kids are going to be safe because the other parent isn't under the influence/ doesn't have any illicit substances in their system.

- It's their way of delaying time between a parent and the child for strategic reasons.

- It's a power play because of the dynamic of the relationship. Maybe the parent insisting on the test wants to put some hurdles in place for the other parent to jump over to test their commitment or simply to make life a bit more challenging.

Whether you decide to do a drug test is a matter for you. I'd encourage getting advice on this from an experienced family lawyer to help you decide.

In considering whether to do a test, you'd want to look to balance doing the test with what you've got to win and lose. You win if it comes back negative; you're seen as committed and willing.

You could lose if it comes back positive for illicit substances. You need to be aware that if you end up in court, your medical records could be subpoenaed, and the result may then be used in court proceedings.

You might, however, see yourself as losing if you do the test because you're giving in to your partner's demands. Your partner might insist you do another one in the future.

What should we consider including in our parenting agreement?

- Parental responsibility

- How often your child is in each parent's care during the school term

- How often your child is in each parent's care during the school holidays

- Special occasions
    - Christmas
    - Easter
    - Special religious or cultural days/events
    - Extended family member special occasions
    - Birthdays – each parent's, each child's
    - Step/half sibling birthdays
    - Mother's Day
    - Father's Day

- Overseas travel

- Passport applications and renewals

- Interstate travel notification

- First option to care for the kids if a parent is unavailable

- Agreed list of carers if a parent is unavailable

- Authority to receive information from your child's school/day care, tutor, treating GP

- Introducing new partners to the kids – a conversation about how and when to introduce

- Having intimate partners stay overnight when the kids are in each parent's care

- Agreed immunisations

- Review date for the care/living arrangements

- Birthday parties

- Birthday and Christmas presents for the kids, each parent, and between the kids

- Not committing kids to an extracurricular activity that may impact a parent's time with them

- Agreement about the kids' bedtimes and/or routines, including mealtimes and diet

- Kids' social media use

- The posting of photos and footage of the kids online (social media and dating profiles)

- Makeup time

- If a parent can't look after the kids during the school holidays when they're scheduled to be in their care, then an arrangement regarding the cost of a school holiday program/babysitting

- COVID vaccinations

Does cheating impact child custody?

No, infidelity by a parent doesn't impact child custody.

That being said, a child's care arrangements after separation must be in the child's best interests. A child's relationship with a parent's new partner can therefore be a relevant factor in what the care arrangements should be.

I represented a dad at court who was the full-time carer of the children. The mum had re-partnered, and the new partner's children bullied my client's kids at school. Needless to say, my client's children didn't want to see their mum in the company of the new partner. Despite this being made clear to the court and the mother, the judge made orders allowing Mum to have time with the children, leaving it up to her to decide if her new partner would be present. The judge was giving her the opportunity to be sensitive to her children's views and needs and not have the partner around. Mum disregarded what the children wanted, and the partner was present when she had the children. This reflected poorly on her.

I don't have permanent housing now. Does that mean I can't have overnights with the kids?

No, not necessarily.

Both you and your partner will want the kids to spend overnights with each of you in a place that is warm, dry, and, importantly, safe. Consider how you can go about facilitating all of these needs – whether that be in a share house, a dad's shelter or even propose that it happen in the family home, with your partner to stay overnight elsewhere.

> ## Guy Advice
>
> *Yeah, it was just difficult to talk to them and try to really build a relationship, I guess. But then once I got through that and got talking, we'd just talk about school and did all that stuff. I had to really build our relationship so they knew I wasn't going anywhere.*

3 PARENTING APPS

There are a range of parenting apps out there to help separated parents effectively communicate with one another and manage their child's care, commitments, and expenses. Some are free, and some are paid subscriptions:

- Our Family Wizard
- 2Houses
- WeParent
- Parentship
- Custody Connection
- FamCal
- Coparenta
- Weparent

- Coparently
- CoPilots
- TimeTree
- MyMob
- Appclose
- TalkingParents
- Peaceful CoParenting
- Fayr – Co-Parenting

Test your knowledge of this chapter by accessing our interactive book at deanpublishing.com/siobhanmullins

CHAPTER 4

Child Support

4

CHILD SUPPORT

INTRODUCTION
WHAT THE LAW SAYS
FAQS

Do I have to pay child support?

Do we have to have a child support assessment?

How can I find out how much child support is without an assessment?

Can a child support assessment be challenged?

What are the reasons why a child support assessment can be challenged?

What is a child support assessment?

Can child support be backdated?

Am I entitled to the Family Tax Benefit A or B if I pay child support?

What is the childcare subsidy?

Am I entitled to the childcare subsidy?

How does child support get paid?

What happens if I don't pay child support?

What happens if my partner is supposed to pay me child support and she doesn't?

Can we agree that neither of us will pay child support to one another?

If our child isn't biologically mine, do I have to pay child support?

If I don't see our child, do I have to pay child support?

Why do I have to pay child support?

If my partner or I have other kids now or in the future, how does that impact the child support assessment?

My partner is only working part-time hours or not at all. Can she be forced to start working or increase her hours?

Can she stop me seeing our kids if I don't pay child support?

Can I withhold child support if she doesn't allow me to see the kids?

What is a non-agency payment?

Can what I've paid in other expenses for the kids be credited towards what I've paid or pay in child support?

What are the different payment kinds that can be credited?

When would the Child Support Agency credit a payment?

My partner drives a car registered in my name. Can the value of my car that she drives be credited towards my child support liability?

REAL LIFE EXAMPLES OF CHILD SUPPORT AGREEMENTS

INTRODUCTION

Child support is a matter that many parents find confusing, difficult to understand, stressful and frustrating.

Some parents assessed to pay child support don't believe in it. They don't believe in it because they think that each parent should be responsible for the kids' costs when they're in their care. And that's right when it comes to, say, housing, utilities, and groceries.

However, it's those extra add-ons, such as school fees, clothing, haircuts, medical appointments, medicines, sports, music lessons, and the like, that they seem to forget someone has to pick up the tab for.

At the crux of this belief is a fear that the child support money they pay the other parent isn't going directly towards their child's benefit. I've heard these parents say that the receiving parent will "piss it up the wall," "not spend it on the kids," that "she'll get another tattoo" or something similar.

For the parent receiving the child support, the problem they face is the other parent "not having a clue about how much the kids' stuff costs." As a result, these parents fear being unable to provide for the kids in a way that they would've if they and the other parent had stayed together.

I share these two views with you so you've got some insight into why you or your partner may be responding in certain ways.

Having to talk money with your partner after separating can become frustrating, tedious, and problematic to your parenting relationship.

When it comes to parents who have a degree of trust in one another, they want some certainty surrounding their financial obligations to the kids. In addition, they want an arrangement that is clean, clear, and easy to follow. So, towards the end of this chapter, I will provide you with some parents' real-life child support agreements.

WHAT THE LAW SAYS

The law says that a child's parents have a duty to financially provide for their kids, whether the kids are biologically theirs or adopted.

The amount of financial support that a parent pays in respect of their kids depends on their and the other parent's income, the children's ages, and the number of overnights the kids are with them for. Other factors can come into play, but these three are used for a child support assessment.

FAQS

Do I have to pay child support?

If there's a child support assessment in place and you're assessed as the parent required to pay, then unless you and your partner agree otherwise – and make this official – the law says yes.

In the absence of a child support assessment, it may be appropriate for you to pay child support to your partner, or vice versa.

Do we have to have a child support assessment?

No, there is no legal requirement to apply for a child support assessment. Some government benefits require a child support administrative assessment to be undertaken though. Generally, Services Australia (aka Centrelink) will do this administrative assessment.

How can I find out how much child support is without an assessment?

Use the online child support estimator to get clear on the approximate amount you may be eligible to receive or required to pay. Visit https://processing.csa.gov.au/estimator/About.aspx

Can a child support assessment be challenged?

Yes. Both you and your partner can challenge a child support assessment.

4

What are the reasons why a child support assessment can be challenged?

There are ten reasons why you or your partner can apply for a child support reassessment:

- The costs of raising the child are significantly affected:
    - By the high costs of spending time or communicating with the child. The costs must be more than five percent of the adjusted taxable income the administrative assessment uses for you and your partner (Reason 1).
    - Because of the child's special needs (Reason 2).
    - Because the child is being cared for, educated, or trained in the way both parents intended (Reason 3).
    - By the parent or non-parent carer's childcare costs when the child is under 12 years (Reason 6).

- The child support assessment is unfair because:
    - Of the child's income, earning capacity, property, or financial resources (Reason 4).
    - You've paid or transferred money, goods or property to your child, the receiving parent or a third party for the child's benefit (Reason 5).
    - Of the income, earning capacity, property, or financial resources of one or both parents (Reason 8).

- Your necessary expenses significantly reduce your capacity to support the child (Reason 7).

- Your capacity to support the child is significantly reduced because there is another person or child to whom you have a duty to maintain, or they have special needs, and the costs associated with spending time or communicating with them are relevant to your capacity (Reason 9).

- Your responsibility to support a resident child significantly reduces your capacity to support another child. (Reason 10)

Any information – excluding personal details if removed by you – or documents that you give to the Child Support Agency to support your application for a reassessment will be given to your partner.

What is a child support assessment?

An assessment describes the calculations used to determine the amount of child support that needs to be paid by each parent.

Can child support be backdated?

Yes, and usually only up to three months worth of backdated child support.

Am I entitled to the Family Tax Benefit A or B if I pay child support?

Potentially, yes, if you care for your child at least 35 percent of the time and subject to other income and residence requirements.

What is the childcare subsidy?

It's a payment made by the Federal Government to approved childcare providers. The provider then passes on the subsidy payment to parents, who pay the difference in the childcare fee.

Am I entitled to the childcare subsidy?

If you and your partner share in your child's care, then potentially, yes. You and your partner would be submitting separate applications for the childcare subsidy.

How does child support get paid?

Pay it between yourselves	Child Support collects it
Cash Pays the other parent in cash.	**BPAY®** Uses phone or internet banking to pay, using the CSA's biller code and the unique reference number.
Bank transfer Pays directly into the other parent's bank account.	**Bank transfer** Transfers the amount into the Agency's bank account, and the Agency pays the other parent.
Employer Arranges for their employer to deduct the amount from their wages. The employer transfers the amount into the other parent's bank account, with the transfer being recorded as "child support."	**Employer** Arranges their employer to deduct the amount from their wage. The employer arranges for the amount to be transferred to the Agency's or the other parent's bank account.

Cheque	Mail
Pays by cheque.	Sends a cheque or money order to the Agency and once cleared, the Agency pays the other parent.
Money order	**Card Payments**
Pays with a money order from Australia Post.	Pays using a credit or debit card, paying online, over the phone, with BillPay or via the Express Plus Child Support mobile app. The Agency then pays the other parent.
	Income support payments
	Has the amount deducted from their income support payments. The Agency then pays the other parent.

What happens if I don't pay child support?

If there is a child support assessment in place, the Child Support Agency can become involved, and any of the following can occur:

1. You can be stopped from leaving Australia if you have a child support debt.

2. Your wages from your employer can be garnished (deducted).

3. Any tax refund that you may be eligible for can be automatically paid to the Child Support Agency and used to pay down your child support debt.

4. You may need to pay a financial penalty.

5. If you're owed money by a government authority, partnership or a society registered or incorporated as a cooperative housing society, they can be required to pay the money owed to you directly to the Child Support Agency. The Child Support Agency may then use this money to pay down your child support debt.

6. Any social security benefit or pension, family tax benefit, age or invalidity pensions, veterans' affairs payments and the like that you receive can be deducted until the child support debt is paid.

7. If you receive a parental leave payment, then this can be deducted until the child support debt is paid.

8. If you're not physically present in Australia, and you generate income from a source within the country in some way shape or form, and another person receives the income on your behalf, then the Child Support Agency can require that person to pay the money to it. The Child Support Agency may then use this money to pay down your child support debt.

9. If satisfied that a transaction was made – for example, the sale of real estate – to defeat payment of your child support liability, then the Child Support Agency can apply to the court to have the sale set aside or the sale proceeds received to pay your child support debt.

10. The absence of child support being paid is a relevant consideration that a judge or judicial officer must consider when making parenting orders.

Please note that the above assumes that you do not otherwise have a formal legal agreement in place regarding child support, for example, a limited child support agreement or a binding child support agreement.

What happens if my partner is supposed to pay me child support and she doesn't?

There can be penalties for not paying child support (as described above). If you have a child support assessment in place, you may want to consider contacting the Child Support Agency to let them know so they can assist with collection.

Can we agree that neither of us will pay child support to one another?

Yes. If you and your partner agree to this, you may want to consider making this agreement official. Read pages 198–199 of Chapter 9 for more detail on this.

If our child isn't biologically mine, do I have to pay child support?

Potentially, yes. Step-parents or adoptive parents may be required to pay child support for their non-biological child.

If I don't see our child, do I have to pay child support?

Yes, if there's a child support assessment or legally binding agreement in place that requires you to pay child support.

Why do I have to pay child support?

Because the law says so.

Our Australian law is supposed to reflect societal values, cultural and social norms and expectations. By and large, our Australian community and the government believe that each parent has a moral obligation to financially provide for the child they brought into the world, regardless of choice and circumstance.

Child support is a means of reducing the burden on the government to financially provide for children and to move the onus of supporting them back onto their parents.

If my partner or I have other kids now or in the future, how does that impact the child support assessment?

If a parent has another child in the future, this can impact a child support assessment.

Income and capacity to financially provide, given the new dependent, are influencing factors in child support assessments. If or when these factors become relevant, the parent wanting to have them reflected in the child support assessment would need to satisfy one of the reassessment grounds.

My partner is only working part-time hours or not at all. Can she be forced to start working or increase her hours?

Your partner can't be forced to start working or increase her hours by the Child Support Agency.

Whether it's appropriate for a child support assessment to be reassessed because of your partner's capacity and ability to work or increase her work hours will be influenced by your child's age and his or her care arrangements.

For example's sake, let's say that your partner worked full-time as a lawyer and your kids lived with you both 50/50, and then your partner stopped working altogether. You could argue that she has a demonstrated capacity to work and earn a decent income and that the child support assessment should be reassessed on that basis. The amount of child support that you'd be assessed to pay may reduce versus your partner being forced by the Child Support Agency itself to return to work as a lawyer.

Can she stop me seeing our kids if I don't pay child support?

Practically, yes. However, not paying child support isn't a basis for withholding the children from a parent.

Can I withhold child support if she doesn't allow me to see the kids?

Practically, yes. However, there can be consequences for you if you withhold child support, particularly if there is a child support assessment in place.

What is a non-agency payment?

It's payment of a child support liability that happens outside of the Child Support Agency between parents.

The parent assessed to pay child support either:

- Pays an amount direct to the other parent

- Pays an amount direct to a third party

- Transfers property to the other parent

- Provides services to the other parent

Can what I've paid in other expenses for the kids be credited towards what I've paid or pay in child support?

Potentially, yes, depending on the payment kind and whether one of these circumstances applies:

1. You and your partner intended for the payment to form part of the child support you're assessed to pay, whether partially or completely.

2. Your official financial separation agreement refers to a non-agency payment being credited towards your child support liability.

3. You have an official child support agreement that deals with non-agency payments.

4. The registrar of the Child Support Agency determines so.

What are the different payment kinds that can be credited?

Payments made by you for the following purposes may be credited towards a child support assessment liability:

- Childcare fees

- Fees charged by a school or preschool for your child

- Amounts payable for school/preschool uniforms and books required for your child

- Fees for essential medical and dental services for your child

Your partner's share of:

- Amounts payable for rent or a security bond for her home

- Amounts payable for utilities, rates or body corporate charges for her home

- Repayments on a loan that financed her home

- Costs to your partner of obtaining and running a vehicle, including repairs and standing costs

When would the Child Support Agency credit a payment?

If you and your partner don't agree to a payment you've made being credited towards your child support liability, then the Child Support Agency may credit the payment up to a maximum of 30 percent if the below is satisfied:

1. If you have made one or more payments to your partner or on their behalf, and

CHILD SUPPORT

2. The payment you're wanting credit for is one of the following kinds:
   a) Childcare fees
   b) Fees charged by a school or preschool for your child
   c) Amounts payable for school/preschool uniforms and books required for your child
   d) Fees for essential medical and dental services for your child
   e) Your partner's share of:
      » Amounts payable for rent or a security bond for her home
      » Amounts payable for utilities, rates or body corporate charges for her home
      » Repayments on a loan that financed her home
   f) Costs to your partner of obtaining and running a vehicle, including repairs and standing costs

7. When you made the payment and when the registrar considered your application to credit the payment(s), you had less than 14 percent care of your child each year, and

8. The total of the payment(s) is more than what's been previously credited towards your child support liability for all past periods, and

9. The payment isn't to make up for a child support debt, and

10. The child support liability hasn't and/or isn't to be fully or partially meet by a lump sum credit

This is called a "non-agency prescribed payment."

For any non-agency payments that you make to be credited, there must be an administrative child support assessment in place.

My partner drives a car registered in my name. Can the value of my car that she drives be credited towards my child support liability?

Potentially, yes, if you and your partner agree or the Child Support Agency determines it is appropriate.

Whilst the car remains in your name, its total value won't be credited towards your child support liability. You and your partner need to agree on an appropriate amount, or the registrar can decide if you're unable to agree.

REAL LIFE EXAMPLES OF CHILD SUPPORT AGREEMENTS

Real-life child support agreement 1:
These parents agreed:

- Dad would pay to Mum child support as assessed.

- They would maintain a joint bank account, which would have $1,000 in it at any given time. They had an agreed list of expenses, and each parent was allowed to use the money in the joint bank account to pay for the kids' expenses when they cropped up.
    » When the funds dropped below $1,000, Mum and Dad would top it up 50/50 to get it back to $1,000.

Real-life child support agreement 2:
These parents agreed:

- One parent would pay a privately agreed amount of child support.

- They would maintain a joint bank account, which would have $500 in it at any given time. They had an agreed list of expenses, and each parent was allowed to use the money in the joint bank account to pay for their child's expenses when they cropped up.
    » Each parent direct deposited $15 per week into the account. If the balance fell below $500, they'd top it back up 50/50.

Real-life child support agreement 3:
These parents agreed:

- Neither of them would pay child support to one another.

- They would maintain a joint bank account, which would have $1,200 in it at any given time. They had an agreed list of expenses, and each parent was allowed to use the money in the joint bank account to pay for their children's expenses when they cropped up.
  - » When the balance of funds in the account fell below $1,200, one parent would pay 100 percent of the amount to top up the account to $1,200.

Real-life child support agreement 4:
These parents agreed:

- Neither of them would pay child support to one another.

- They would maintain a joint bank account, which would have $600 in it at any given time. They had an agreed list of expenses, and each parent was allowed to use the money in the joint bank account to pay for their children's agreed expenses when they cropped up.

» When the balance of funds in the account fell below $600, the dad would top it up 60 percent, and the mum would top it up 40 percent.

Test your knowledge of this chapter by accessing our interactive book at deanpublishing.com/siobhanmullins

Siobhan is sharing more in her INTERACTIVE book.

See exclusive downloads, videos, audios and photos.

DOWNLOAD it now at deanpublishing.com/siobhanmullins

CHAPTER 5

Your Financial Split (Property Settlement)

5

YOUR FINANCIAL SPLIT (PROPERTY SETTLEMENT)

INTRODUCTION

WHAT THE LAW SAYS

WORKING OUT THE FINANCIAL SPLIT

REAL LIFE

INFORMATION SHARING

FAQS

- Is 50/50 fair?
- What is a fair split?
- Is there a maths formula for working out what a fair split is?
- Do women always get more of the assets than men?
- Are our kids' care arrangements relevant to our financial split?
- Why are our kids' care arrangements relevant to our financial split?
- If my partner is working part-time or not at all, how relevant is that to our financial split?
- Can my partner force me to sell the house (or other assets) if I want to explore keeping it?
- Is what I owned before our relationship classed as mine free and clear (excluded)?
- What date does everything (the pie) get split at?
- I want to keep all my super. Can I do that?
- Do we have to split super?
- How should we split super?
- How do we work out a super-cash trade-off amount?
- Do I have to pay maintenance?
- Can my partner be required to pay me maintenance?
- Does she have to give me her financial information?
- When is a loan considered a gift?
- Do I have to pay stamp duty on my partner's share if she transfers the house/car/shares to me?
- Do we have to pay capital gains tax if we transfer the house/cars/shares?
- Are we entitled to each other's future inheritances?
- My partner/I received an inheritance after we separated. Am I/is she entitled to any of it?
- Is my partner entitled to any of the inheritance that I received when we were together?
- Can we divorce without a financial separation agreement?
- If we make our financial separation agreement official, can we change it in the future if we both agree?
- What happens to our original official financial separation agreement if we get back together in the future and then separate again?
- Is a property settlement taxable income?
- Can my partner make a claim on anything that I've bought, received, saved, won, or inherited after we separated?
- How are debts incurred after separation treated?
- How are individual debts incurred when we were together treated?
- We're not married. Does that make any difference to our financial split?
- How does splitting super work?
- Am I entitled to my partner's super?
- Are wedding bands and engagement rings included?
- Are household contents valued at insurance or garage sale value?
- Is cheating relevant to our financial split?
- What is a resource?

INTRODUCTION

Working out the financial aspect of separation (aka the property settlement) tends to be the most stressful and overwhelming for many people. My team and I field more questions about the financial aspects of separating than we do about parenting, indicating that people feel more confident in working that aspect out with their partner.

The most frequently asked question is, "Where do I start?"

I encourage people to start by getting clear on what's already agreed or likely to be agreed. I call this the "Safe Assumptions Exercise." In doing this, you narrow the issues you and your partner must decide, reducing overwhelm and stress.

The next part of this exercise is outsourcing what you don't know, for example, the value of what you own in cars, real estate, contents, debts, superannuation and more. In reality, you and your partner are unlikely to be experts in values, so outsourcing to a third party or using verifiable sources (such as bank statements) means you and your partner spend less time on disputing items' values.

The Safe Assumptions Exercise, with values, is relevant to what I'm about to share below.

If you want to learn my method for helping couples reach a financial separation agreement, read my book, *Splitting Up Together: The How-To Handbook for an AMICABLE Divorce*. This handbook breaks down the process and steps from start to finish, following my AMICABLE method, which is an acronym, to separate, reach an agreement and make it all official.

5 WHAT THE LAW SAYS

When it comes to working out a financial split, there are two legal approaches that can be adopted:

- A global approach – combining all assets, debts, and super together to assess how each person contributed to the total pie

- An asset-by-asset approach – assessing how each person contributed to each individual asset

The global approach is more popular. Sometimes, depending on the nature of the assets or super, it might be appropriate to treat a particular asset separate from the global approach, for example, a superannuation interest already in the pension payment phase or an inheritance received after separation. Another instance might be if a couple informally split their finances after separating, delayed making that agreement official and went on to build more wealth individually. It may be appropriate for that new wealth to be dealt with separately versus as part of the global approach.

Lawyers and judges talk about the "pool": the non-super pool, the super pool, and the global pool. These pools summarise the total cash, cars, real estate, shares, businesses, cryptocurrency, contents, home loans, personal loans, credit card debts, superannuation, and trusts you and your partner have in your joint and separate names.

I like to keep it simple and call the pool "pie." It's easier to conceptualise because you and your partner each get a piece.

For couples closer to retirement, it may be preferable to assess contributions and future needs for the total pie, therefore adopting a one pie approach.

For couples further away from retiring and accessing their super, it's generally more appropriate to have two pies, assessing future needs and contributions to the non-super and then the super pie.

The non-super pie
(aka the non-superannuation pool)

The super pie
(aka the superannuation pool)

The total pie combined non-super + super pies
(the global pool)

5

WORKING OUT THE FINANCIAL SPLIT

The law says to get clear on what is an appropriate financial split of the pie after a couple separate, there are four steps.

- **Step 1:** Identify the pie – that is, all the assets, debts, superannuation, and resources and values that exist now in joint and individual names.

- **Step 2:** Assess each person's contributions to the pie, which includes all non-financial, financial, domestic, and parenting contributions.

- **Step 3:** Consider each person's future needs.

- **Step 4:** Determine whether the overall financial split is appropriate – is it just and equitable?

People can get more or less of the pie at steps two, three and four.

It might be appropriate for someone to receive more of the pie at step two to recognise their greater contribution. That greater contribution might be, for example, because of the assets that person brought into the relationship, the inheritance received (and its application to the pie), or the sacrifice or role they had during the relationship. Alternatively, contributions might be assessed as roughly the same.

It might be appropriate for someone to receive more of the pie at step three to recognise their greater future needs. Those future needs might be due to, for example, their lower income, their age (being closer to retirement than their partner) or because they'll have greater care of the kids. Alternatively, future needs might be assessed as roughly the same.

> ### Guy Advice
>
> *Basically, I knew what I wanted. I wanted to keep my business side of it. She never really had a lot to do with it anyway. I basically said to her, "Write a list. Tell me what you would like, and then we can go from there." I thought that was the easiest way to do it. Give her the option to come up with an outcome.*

REAL LIFE

I know you're probably after a clear formula to help you work out who should get what. The thing is that family law is very grey and discretionary. There's no hard and fast rule and no legal calculation. There is always a range as to what is an appropriate, just and equitable outcome. Family law works off ranges guided by legal principles rather than specifics.

For example, if you go to see an experienced family lawyer for advice, you can expect they might say to you something along the lines of, "An outcome that sees you receive 40-50 percent of the non-super pool would be within the range of a just and equitable outcome."

You hear about those 70/30 or 90/10 splits of the non-super pie where it's small, and there's a primary carer. When I say small, I'm talking less than $500,000 making up the non-super pie.

- Most of the couples whom we work with, regardless of whether they have kids together, end up with an agreement that falls in the 40-60 percent split range of the total pie (the total value of the non-super and super pies combined).

- Our female clients have opted to receive more of the non-super pie and forgo more in super, and our male clients have opted to receive more in super and forgo more of the non-super pie.

- We've seen an increasing trend with couples doing cash-super trade-offs. Sometimes people prefer to keep their super intact and take less of the non-super assets. For others, they prefer to be able to afford to keep the family home by taking more of the non-super pie and less super.

Guy Advice

I said something mean to her when we separated. When she threw some really large figures around, I said, "What? So, you came with nothing, and you want to leave with everything?" That's what I threw at her. And it was just ... Yeah, it was probably the meanest thing I said to her the whole time. But I didn't want her to leave with nothing. I wanted her to be able to set herself up. So, I threw some numbers at her, and I said, "If you do it right, you'll have all this extra money within 12 months. You'll be able to buy another house if you want to do that, if that's what your goal is."

INFORMATION SHARING

You and your partner are legally required to exchange information with one another about your finances. This means providing all tax returns, payslips, bank transaction and credit card statements, share statements, super statements, appraisals, proof of debts and more. This is called a full and frank financial disclosure obligation.

You've got to do it. There's no point refusing to provide documents or trying to hide assets.

If you or your partner refuse to exchange information, it might be a stumbling block to you reaching an agreement. It can also mean that if you don't exchange the required information and you do reach an agreement, your agreement can be challenged in the future. You therefore won't have peace of mind that what you own, inherit, save, accrue, and receive in the future is yours free and clear to keep.

5 FAQS

Is 50/50 fair?

First question, 50 percent of what? Next question, fair to who? Next question, fair according to who or what?

There is no legal presumption that 50/50 is the starting point or fair.

What is a fair split?

It depends on your family's circumstances. I've identified the considerations guiding appropriate financial splits according to the law.

You need to step away from using the term "fair" though. Fair is a subjective term. It means different things to different people. Whenever I've asked people, "Fair according to who?", they say, "According to the law." My response has been, "If the law said you get 99 percent, would you say that's fair?" Their response, "No." I say, "Well, what if your partner gets 99 percent, would you say that's fair?" Their response, "No."

Percentages are useless without context. People say, "We want a 50/50 split." My response is always, "Of what?" And it may turn out to be just the equity available in the home, for example. In the eyes of the law, including all assets, debts and super, it could equate more to a 60/40 split.

Replace the word "fair" with "appropriate."

Is there a maths formula for working out what a fair split is?

No, there is no prescribed maths formula for working out what a fair financial split is.

Lawyers and family court judges use calculations to get a feel for what value a gift, contribution and/or income difference has in the context of the pie. However, this is to get a general feel for the dollar value and its impact in percentage terms. This calculation can result in an adjustment – that is, a person receiving more or less of the pie.

Do women always get more of the assets than men?

No.

Are our kids' care arrangements relevant to our financial split?

Yes, it's just one consideration though among a whole list of others.

Why are our kids' care arrangements relevant to our financial split?

Because if a child or children are living primarily or full-time with one parent, then that parent will likely need more of the pie to accommodate them.

For example, they'll need more space than the other parent. They may also need to reduce their work hours to care for a child or the kids, which then impacts their career, leave entitlements and income earning capacity.

And depending on the level of financial support the other parent provides, which might be the bare minimum or absolutely everything, the primary parent could expect to pick up all of those incidental costs, thereby having a greater financial burden than the other parent.

If my partner is working part-time or not at all, how relevant is that to our financial split?

One of the factors that is considered when determining an appropriate financial split is each person's income and any gap that exists. The reasons why your partner is working part-time or not at all would likely influence the weight that's attached to any adjustment to you or your partner because of your individual incomes.

For example, your children's care arrangements or their ages might impact your partner's ability to work or commit to full-time hours. Similarly, your partner's health, whether she's studying and/or can work in her profession due to location, are relevant considerations. These considerations are distinct, though, from lifestyle choices.

Can my partner force me to sell the house (or other assets) if I want to explore keeping it?

A person has the right to reasonably explore keeping an asset when they have the possible financial capacity to do so and/or such an outcome may very well contribute to an appropriate outcome overall.

Is what I owned before our relationship classed as mine free and clear (excluded)?

No, not necessarily.

What date does everything (the pie) get split at?

The strict legal approach says the current date.

Why? Because people can make after-separation contributions that increase or reduce the pie through their actions. Their circumstances can change after they separate, and it might be inappropriate and therefore unfair if what existed at the time of separation, versus the current date, was what got split.

I recently worked with a couple that separated in February 2020. Part of their agreement included the wife keeping the home and making a payment to the husband equal to 50 percent of the equity. They came to see me in November 2021 to make their agreement official.

- In February 2020, the house was worth $975,000.

- In November 2020, the house was worth $1.03 million.

- In November 2021, the house was worth $1.33 million. That's a jump of $355,000 in 21 months.

This is just one example where it would have been inappropriate to run with the February 2020 house value because, essentially, this value increase was brought about through circumstance – the booming property market –and not by any specific action of either of them. Consider the flipside of this. The share market falling through is neither person's fault.

All that being said, many couples agree to crystallise the

value of some or all of their assets, debts and super at the time that they separated, and that's fine to do as long as the overall agreement is considered appropriate in the eyes of the law. This notion is only possible in the separation agreement space though. It doesn't generally happen if you or your partner ask a judge to decide your financial split for you.

I want to keep all my super. Can I do that?

Yes, if you and your partner agree and if the proposed overall financial split is fair in the eyes of the law (assuming you want to make your agreement official).

If you and your partner don't agree on a financial split and you need to go to court, superannuation is up for grabs, so to speak, and a Judge may very well split your super, even if you don't want that to happen.

Do we have to split super?

No, there is no legal requirement to split superannuation.

How should we split super?

This answer is best explained by watching a four minute explainer video. Scan the QR code to watch now.

How do we work out a super-cash trade-off amount?

There's no hard and fast rule on this. Generally speaking, though, subject to each person's age, a cash-super trade off does involve some discounting because cash is seen as more valuable than super, as you can use it immediately.

I've seen couples work out the super-cash trade-off by first agreeing in principle on the split of their non-super pie and their super pie. They then compare the amount of superannuation to be split and deduct or adjust that against the non-super pie.

To give an example, I worked with a couple where the wife was going to keep the home, refinance the home loan and make a payment to the husband. The wife was a public servant; the husband was a small business owner, who hadn't paid himself much super during their relationship.

The husband and wife worked out that there'd need to be a split of the wife's superannuation to the husband. The couple identified the amount of super that'd need to be split from the wife's super to the husband, which was about $130,000. The wife wanted to keep as much of her super as possible, so they looked at the non-super pie to adjust for this.

The husband and wife agreed that instead of the husband getting $130,000 from the wife's super, he'd get an extra $100,000 cash from the non-super pie, plus whatever else he was already going to keep in exchange for the wife keeping the home. They each then kept their own super.

Note: This is an example only of what a couple agreed to without any legal advice.

Do I have to pay maintenance?

If you have an official agreement or a judge's order requiring you to pay maintenance, then yes.

That being said, in the lead up to you getting an official agreement or a judge ordering you to pay maintenance, it may be appropriate for you to pay interim maintenance, just until your financial split is sorted. Maintenance doesn't necessarily have to be you paying money to your partner directly; it could be paying expenses on her behalf, for example, the lease repayments for the car she drives or the home loan.

Whether maintenance is relevant to you and your partner will depend on need and capacity.

Can my partner be required to pay me maintenance?

Potentially, yes.

Does she have to give me her financial information?

Yes, your partner (like you) is under a legal obligation to provide information to you about her financial circumstances. This includes payslips, tax returns, appraisals, bank statements, share statements, superfund member statements, lease agreements and the like.

When is a loan considered a gift?

The following considerations are relevant to determining whether money given is to be considered a loan or a gift:

1. The existence of any loan documentation around the time of the supposed loan being paid

2. Whether there is or was an arrangement or agreement regarding payment terms, interest, and/or a schedule of payments for the supposed loan

3. Whether a person made any repayments on the supposed loan

4. Each person's knowledge of the supposed loan

5. Whether there was a deadline or due date for repayment of the supposed loan

6. Whether there were any conditions attached to the supposed loan

7. Whether the loan was secured in any way

8. The representations, if any, made to any organisations or professionals

Do I have to pay stamp duty on my partner's share if she transfers the house/car/shares to me?

If the transfer is made because of an official financial separation agreement or relevant court order, then no, stamp duty will not be payable. There is a concession or exemption that applies.

Do we have to pay capital gains tax if we transfer the house/cars/shares?

If the transfer is made because of an official financial separation agreement or relevant court order, then no, a capital gains tax event will not be triggered. You'll be able to transfer the house/cars/shares without having to pay capital gains tax, as rollover relief applies.

The person receiving the house/cars/shares will inherit the cost base of the asset. When they're ready to sell the asset, then capital gains tax may be payable then.

You should confirm this information with your accountant or lawyer in case the law changes or your assets are unique.

Are we entitled to each other's future inheritances?

If you and your partner make your financial separation agreement official or a judge makes orders about your financial split, then strictly speaking, no, your partner is not entitled to your future inheritance and vice versa.

A legally-binding agreement or order made under our Family Law Act 1975 will mean that what is yours will remain yours into the future. The same goes for your partner.

Warning though – for this to be true, both you and your partner must disclose all your finances. You've got to put it all on the table and share information about what you own in assets, super and any other resources, and what you owe in debts. If you or your partner don't, then one of you can challenge the official agreement or orders.

My partner/I received an inheritance after we separated. Am I/is she entitled to any of it?

It's not so much that the other person will get some of the inheritance received after separating, but rather an adjustment may be made in their favour in the split of the non-super pie to see the person who received the inheritance keep it.

Sometimes people will put the inheritance in a separate pie so there's three: the non-super pie, the super pie, and the inheritance pie. You're best to get legal advice on the specific answer to this question.

Is my partner entitled to any of the inheritance that I received when we were together?

The answer is that it depends. But it's not so much an "entitlement" to the inheritance; it's more nuanced than that.

People receive inheritances in the form of cash, cars, shares, or real estate. Sometimes people will sell their inheritance, thereby changing its nature. Then, the cash received from the inheritance might be absorbed into the pie.

Depending on the value of the inheritance you received, when it was received, and what was done with it, there may be an adjustment (a swing) in your favour to say you ought to get a bit more of the pie to account for this contribution.

Can we divorce without a financial separation agreement?

Yes. Divorcing will start a 12-month time limit within which you must either reach a financial separation agreement and make it official or, if you don't have an agreement, apply to the court for a judge to decide for you.

If we make our financial separation agreement official, can we change it in the future if we both agree?

Potentially, yes. Only in certain circumstances – and if a couple agrees – can official financial separation agreements be changed.

I worked with a couple to make their financial separation agreement official. Less than 12 months later, they returned wanting to add an extra part to their agreement to include a split of the husband's superannuation to the wife. We successfully made this happen. This was possible because they agreed.

What happens to our original official financial separation agreement if we get back together in the future and then separate again?

If you and your partner get back together and separate for a second time, it is possible for your original financial separation agreement to be changed or discharged.

Financial separation agreements made official in a financial consent order can only be changed or discharged in very limited circumstances.

Depending on your and your partner's circumstances at the time of the second separation, along with some other factors, you might need to simply do a second financial separation agreement dealing with your finances at the time of the second separation. Essentially, you and your partner could:

1. Agree to new Financial Consent Orders

2. Agree to enter a binding financial agreement

3. If you don't agree, apply to the court for a decision about the original financial consent orders and resolve the current division of finances

Below are some considerations that would be arguably relevant to what should happen with the original official financial separation agreement:

- Whether at the time of making your original financial separation agreement official you both intended for it to sever your financial ties together for all time.

- The time between making the original financial separation agreement official and when you and your partner got back together

- How long you and your partner were together for the second time before again separating

- Whether you and your partner abided by and carried out the terms from the original financial separation agreement

- How you and your partner managed your finances after getting back together, for example, how housing, day-to-day living costs, groceries, utilities, and the like were paid for, and the degree that you intermingled your finances

- Whether you and your partner purchased or acquired any assets or debts for joint or individual purposes

Is a property settlement taxable income?

No.

Can my partner make a claim on anything that I've bought, received, saved, won, or inherited after we separated?

Yes, potentially.

How are debts incurred after separation treated?

Noting that the law says the pie is split at the current date, debts incurred after separation are included in the pie to be divided between you and your partner.

The reasonableness of those debts, however, and whether they should be included can be a point of argument. For example, you or your partner using a credit card to pay $700 to replace the tyres on a car is arguably reasonable versus, say, paying $30,000 for a new fridge.

How are individual debts incurred when we were together treated?

The general proposition is that the debts are shared. However, the purpose of the debts, the amount owing, how the debt was acquired, and whether a person knew about the debts are all relevant factors that the law says require consideration.

For some couples, judges have determined one person should receive a reduced financial split because of their gambling or deliberate, intentional, or reckless decisions that have reduced the pie available for division.

We're not married. Does that make any difference to our financial split?

No. The legal principles for married and de facto couples are extremely similar if not the same. The specific provisions are just dealt with under separate sections of our Family Law Act 1975.

How does splitting super work?

1. First off, your financial separation agreement is either made official, or a relevant court makes orders about your financial split, which includes a superannuation split.

2. The superfund trustee must be provided (served) with the official agreement or court orders.

3. The person receiving the super split (the non-member) must provide some information to the superfund about themselves, for example, contact details and tax file number.

4. The superfund will then split the amount from the member's super balance and:
    - Set it aside in an account within the same fund in the non-member's name or
    - Roll the super split amount out to the non-member's superfund choice.

Whether the super split amount can remain within the same superfund will depend on the superfund's rules.

If the member's super is already in the payment phase, then the non-member may begin to receive a pension payment from the super amount split to them. If the member isn't yet receiving the super, then the amount split to the non-member remains in the non-member's super account until they satisfy the requirements to access their super.

Am I entitled to my partner's super?

An entitlement is a right to have what's being put or proposed considered, so yes.

Whether in all the circumstances it's appropriate for you to receive some of your partner's super is a different exercise. The same goes for your partner too.

Are wedding bands and engagement rings included?

Yes, they can be. Some couples ignore the value of these items altogether though. Remember, in the family law world, it's not the insurance value that is adopted, rather the market value.

Guy Advice

It's gonna sound funny, but I wanted the entertainment unit where we put the TV. That's the only thing I wanted because I got a room that I wanted to set that up in. I said to her, "You got everything else, but I want that." But in the end, I gave up on that too. Yeah, I just gave up. It wasn't worth the fight for a $600 entertainment unit. I got to a point where I just thought, let's keep things amicable, and it was 50/50 minus 600 bucks.

Are household contents valued at insurance or garage sale value?

Garage sale value, because there is no clearer or more objective evidence as to an item's value than what the target market is willing to pay.

Is cheating relevant to our financial split?

No. In Australia we have a no-fault divorce system, meaning that neither person is penalised in the financial split at the end of their relationship if there is infidelity.

What is a resource?

A resource is something to do with the future, that mightn't be capable of being split, or is income-generating. For example:

- Long service leave

- Annual leave

- Future inheritances where you or your partner are named as a beneficiary of the estate and:
    - The will maker has died.
    - The will maker's death is imminent.
    - The will maker has lost capacity to change their will.

- A DVA pension

- Income generating assets

- You/your partner have a pending compensation/damages claim, whether that be for a motor vehicle accident, victims of crime, workplace injury or other

- You/your partner have a pending disability insurance claim

- You/your partner have pending court proceedings where you may be compensated

- You/your partner are a beneficiary of a trust

- You/your partner are entitled to receive income from an income generating asset or draw money from an asset

- A life interest in real estate

- Previous tax losses that can be offset against future income

Test your knowledge of this chapter by accessing our interactive book at deanpublishing.com/siobhanmullins

CHAPTER 6

Maintenance

6

MAINTENANCE

INTRODUCTION

WHAT THE LAW SAYS

FAQS

Why is maintenance a thing after separation?

Do I have to pay maintenance to my partner?

Can my partner be required to pay me maintenance?

How long does maintenance get paid for?

What if my partner gets married or starts living with a new partner – do I have to continue paying maintenance?

What if my partner isn't working – how does that come into maintenance?

What can maintenance look like?

INTRODUCTION

Maintenance (what Americans term "alimony") is financial support by a person to the other after separation.

Maintenance involves a two-part test:

Person A
has a reasonable need:

Person A's income - (minus) Person A's individual expenses

If - = **reasonable need**

If + = no reasonable need

AND:

Person B
has capacity:

Person B's income - (minus) Person B's individual expenses

If + = **capacity**

If - = no capacity

How is the maintenance amount calculated? It's a numbers exercise based on each person's income and personal expenses. For example, if Jill's shortfall was $50 per week and Jack's buffer was $100, Jack may only be assessed to pay the shortfall of $50 per week, not necessarily $100.

Considerations to note:

- When working out Person A's income, Centrelink benefits and child support payments are excluded.

- When working out whether Person B has capacity, their obligations to pay child support are included as part of their individual expenses.

- Expenses relating to children, for example, utilities, petrol, food, and the like, are apportioned so it's not 100 percent of the adult's individual expenses, even though that adult likely pays for it all.

6
MAINTENANCE

At the end of the day, calculating an appropriate amount of maintenance to be paid is an art not a science. Getting a general feel for the preceding 12 months average living expenses is indicative of need and capacity. If you and your partner begin to live separately and apart in different homes, then some future financial projections would inevitably come into play too when it comes to need and capacity.

Need an easy-to-use budget calculator to determine your potential need or capacity for maintenance? Scan the QR code to be taken to Moneysmart's budget planner.

WHAT THE LAW SAYS

The law sets out some factors that can be considered when determining whether it's appropriate for maintenance to be paid.

A summary of the factors for you and your partner that are considered include:

- Age and health status

- Physical and mental capacity to be appropriately and gainfully employed

- Income, property, and resources

- Care arrangements for a child of the relationship (under 18 years)

- Commitments to support oneself, a child, or another person where there is a duty to maintain, that is, financially support

- A responsibility to support any other person

- Any pension, benefit, or allowance that you/your partner are eligible for (including from super) and the amount

- A standard of living that is reasonable in all the circumstances

- Whether a person would be enabled to undertake education, training or self-establish in a business to obtain an adequate income if maintenance were paid

- If there is a creditor (someone who is owed money), then the effect of a proposed maintenance order on that creditor to recover the money, if relevant

- How the proposed maintenance recipient has contributed to the other person's income, earning capacity, property, and financial resources

- The duration of the relationship and the extent to which it has affected the earning capacity of the proposed maintenance recipient

- The need to protect a person who wishes to continue their role as a parent

- If you/your partner are living with someone, then the financial circumstances relating to the cohabitation

- The terms of any order made or proposed to be made on your/your partner's property or, if relevant, a bankruptcy

- The terms of any order or declaration made or proposed to be made in relation to either of you, your/your partner's new partner, the property owned by you/your partner or, if relevant, a bankruptcy

- Child support that has been or is to be provided or might be liable to be paid for a child of the relationship

- Any fact or circumstance that the justice of the case requires to be considered

- The terms of any binding financial agreement between you and your partner

FAQS

Why is maintenance a thing after separation?

Because decisions made for the sake of a relationship, or just life events, can negatively impact a person's ability to work, progress their career, and earn an income equivalent to their experience, education, and qualifications.

Examples of these impactful decisions and events include moving interstate or overseas for someone's career, having kids and taking time off work to raise them, a child's health, their care and living arrangements, and you or your partner's health.

Do I have to pay maintenance to my partner?

No – unless you and your partner agree, or a judge orders you to.

Can my partner be required to pay me maintenance?

Potentially, yes. This goes back to the maintenance test, what you and your partner agree or, failing agreement, what a judge orders.

How long does maintenance get paid for?

It depends; there is no hard and fast time limit.

Our laws recognise that it's in a separated couple's best interests for them to cut all financial ties insofar as possible and sooner rather than later. For most couples where maintenance is to be paid, a couple will agree to a time limit or income threshold and if there's no agreement, a judge decides for them.

Couples I've worked with have agreed to maintenance being stopped altogether or gradually reduced in the following scenarios:

- When their youngest child starts kindergarten, enabling the primary carer to start work or increase their work hours

- Once a person completes their qualification, which will then assist them to obtain employment in their field and self-support

- As a person's income reaches a certain amount each year

What if my partner gets married or starts living with a new partner – do I have to continue paying maintenance?

If your partner gets married, unless there are special circumstances, an order for spouse maintenance to continue to be paid will stop. If there are court orders in place requiring you to pay your partner maintenance, then you need to apply to the court to vary the maintenance orders. If the maintenance requirement is documented in a Binding Financial Agreement (BFA), consider getting legal advice first before stopping payment altogether.

If your partner starts living with a new partner, then you may still need to continue paying maintenance. You'll need to get advice on this from an experienced family lawyer, as the proper answer will depend on your and your partner's circumstances at the time.

What if my partner isn't working – how does that come into maintenance?

The reasons behind why your partner isn't working will be relevant.

Your partner's health, how long she's not worked for, her trained area of expertise, where she's living, job prospects, and care arrangements for any children of the relationship who are under 18 years are all relevant considerations.

What can maintenance look like?

Maintenance doesn't necessarily have to be a person handing over cash or making direct deposits. Maintenance can look like paying expenses on a person's behalf. For example, car loan repayments for a car that Person A drives or the cost of a private health insurance policy that includes Person A on the policy.

Test your knowledge of this chapter by accessing our interactive book at deanpublishing.com/siobhanmullins

6

MAINTENANCE

Guy Advice

I wish one of my mates just pulled me aside and said, "What are you doing?" You know? Like an outside person saying, "Pull your head in. Why are you even doing this? Why are you considering separating?" I think the biggest thing, I guess, it's not a regret, but we didn't go to the extreme and all of a sudden jump out and say, "I'm out. I'm renting an apartment because I'm not staying with you." We were able to control our emotions and deal with each other. Like, I suppose me being away a fair bit helped. But we didn't go waste a heap of money that we didn't need to. Like, yeah, so it's not a regret, it's a positive, I guess, if you can try and do that. I don't know, is that helpful?

CHAPTER 7

Divorce

7 DIVORCE

INTRODUCTION

FAQS

When can we apply for divorce?

Why do we have to wait 12 months and a day to apply for divorce?

Do we have to divorce?

What's the difference between applying for divorce by myself or applying with my partner jointly?

Does my partner have to consent to getting divorced?

Can I object to a divorce order being issued?

What's the process to get divorced?

Can a divorce order be rescinded?

What grounds can I object to a divorce order being issued?

What are the divorce requirements?

What does a divorce actually do?

Is it better for us to stay married or divorce after we separate?

What is an annulment?

What is the legal definition of "separation"?

We've been married for less than two years. Can we get divorced?

7

DIVORCE

INTRODUCTION

Divorce is for those married couples whose marriage has irretrievably ended, and they want their legal relationship as a married couple to come to an end from a legal perspective.

Divorce is a separate matter from your finances (property settlement), maintenance, parenting, and child support. There's no requirement for you ever to divorce, but it can be a good idea from a practical standpoint.

7 FAQS

When can we apply for divorce?

12 months and one day after the date you separate.

Why do we have to wait 12 months and a day to apply for divorce?

Because many couples get back together within 12 months of separating.

Do we have to divorce?

No, there is no legal requirement to divorce.

What's the difference between applying for divorce by myself or applying with my partner jointly?

	Joint Application	Solo Application
Number of Applicants	2	1
Paperwork required to be served on spouse	No	Yes
Proof of service for paperwork on spouse required	No	Yes
Court attendance required	No	Yes – if there is a child under 18 years

We offer a Joint Application for Divorce Playbook, which breaks down the process, steps, and how-to instructions for applying jointly for a divorce. Scan the QR code to get the playbook.

Does my partner have to consent to getting divorced?

No.

Can I object to a divorce order being issued?

Yes.

What's the process to get divorced?

1. Prepare the required divorce application paperwork.

2. Sign the required divorce application.

3. Submit the required divorce application and supporting documents to the court online via the

Commonwealth Courts Portal. A divorce hearing date is allocated immediately after you submit the paperwork, which is generally about 4-6 weeks into the future. If a person applies for divorce by themselves, they must arrange for their spouse to be served (given) the divorce paperwork.

4. The divorce hearing occurs. If all requirements are satisfied, the court approves the divorce.

5. The divorce order takes effect and becomes available for download from the Commonwealth Court's Portal 30 days after the divorce hearing. If there are special circumstances where this would be appropriate, the court can cause the divorce order to take effect before 30 days.

Can a divorce order be rescinded?

Yes, in the following circumstances:

1. Where a couple gets back together in between the divorce order being approved and the divorce order taking effect

2. Where there has been a miscarriage of justice due to fraud, perjury, suppression of evidence or any other circumstance

If you or your partner die after the divorce hearing and before the divorce order takes effect (being 30 days after the divorce hearing), then the divorce order cannot take effect.

What grounds can I object to a divorce order being issued?

Grounds for objecting to a divorce order being issued are:

1. Your partner submitted their divorce application before you'd been separated for 12 months and one day; or

2. There's a chance you and your partner will get back together (from both your perspectives); or

3. The court doesn't have jurisdiction to determine the divorce application.

What are the divorce requirements?

For a divorce order to be granted by the court, you must:

1. Be validly married

2. Be separated for at least 12 months and one day

3. If you have a child under 18 years, satisfy the court that there are appropriate care arrangements in place for them

4. Satisfy the court that there is no reasonable likelihood of you and your spouse getting back together.

At least one of you must be an Australian citizen, consider Australia to be your permanent home or be an ordinary resident of Australia in the 12 months before submitting the divorce application.

7

What does a divorce actually do?

A divorce does a few things:

1. Ends your relationship as a married couple from a legal perspective.

2. Starts a 12-month time limit within which you must either:
   a) Reach a financial separation agreement and make it official or
   b) If you don't have an agreement, apply to the court for a decision on a financial split.

3. If you haven't made a maintenance agreement official, then it'll start a 12-month time limit within which you must either:
   a) Reach a maintenance agreement and make it official or
   b) If you don't have an agreement and one of you needs maintenance, then apply to the court for maintenance.

4. If you have a will, then depending on your jurisdiction, any gifts that you and your partner made to one another can be automatically rescinded, that is, struck through. The gifts aren't given to your partner. Instead, the gifts are returned to the estate and distributed to any other named beneficiaries.

Is it better for us to stay married or divorce after we separate?

Some people decide to remain married and not divorce. Some reasons include:

- Being able to remain on the same private health fund insurance policy.
    - Certain health funds will require separated and divorced couples to maintain separate insurance policies, which can add an extra cost.

- The time, money, and effort in updating their estate plan.
    - Depending on which jurisdiction you're in, a divorce will either mean that your will is invalid altogether or if you've given any gifts to your partner under your will, then the gift is invalidated. The gift goes back into your estate to be distributed in the terms set out in the rest of the will.

- For tax.
    - In submitting your individual tax returns, married couples still need to disclose their spouse's income. This information can be used by the ATO to calculate your private health insurance rebate, your entitlement to any seniors or pensions tax offset or Medicare levy reduction, or if you need to pay a Medicare levy surcharge.

- Emotional reasons.
  - Sometimes people aren't emotionally ready to end their legal relationship as a married couple, or sometimes people feel there is the potential for them and their partner to get back together.

- Their children.
  - Some parents view having their marriage remain intact and them not being divorced as being better and easier for their kids.

- Religious or cultural reasons.
  - Religious reasons might prevent a person from taking the formal legal step of divorcing. In some cultures, the shame and stigma of being divorced may also stop someone from divorcing.

- Time and effort.
  - Sometimes people just can't be bothered with sorting out the legal paperwork to apply for a divorce. This is generally a short-term reason, and eventually, after the dust has settled, people are more inclined to apply for divorce.

- Can't afford the divorce application filing fee.
  - This is generally a short-term reason because the court's filing fee is a significant upfront cost. At the time of writing this book, the divorce application filing fee is $990.

- Superannuation death beneficiary payout tax free.
  - You can still be considered your partner's dependent for superannuation purposes, meaning that you could be eligible to receive her superannuation.

- Time limitation.
    - With no divorce order, there are no time limits on you and your partner making your financial and maintenance separation agreements official.

Some reasons for divorcing include:

- Capital gains tax.
    - Married couples can only have one principal place of residence. If each person owns a home, then one or both residences could attract a capital gains tax liability that's to be paid when the home is sold.

- Emotional.
    - Divorce can be the emotional closure that some people need to finalise all aspects of their relationship.

- Financial.
    - Divorce starts the 12-month time limit within which financial and maintenance separation agreements must be reached and made official, or if there's no agreement, then court proceedings started. Such a time limit can add pressure on people to progress these matters if they're dragging their feet, or it can provide peace of mind that there's an end to their financial relationship.

- It's cleaner from an estate planning perspective.
    - Depending on which jurisdiction you're in, a divorce will either mean that your will is invalid altogether or if you've given any gifts to your partner under your will, then the gift is invalid.

- It's easier to argue that your partner is not a legal dependent, so it's then easier (subject to jurisdiction) for your superannuation to fall directly into your estate to be dealt with in the terms of your will.

- Remarrying.
    - If you or your partner are officially divorced, then you can legally remarry.

What is an annulment?

An annulment is an invalidation of a marriage. Speaking plainly, there are two different types of annulments:

- Legal annulment – the marriage that occurred was invalid for legal reasons.

- Religious annulment – the conditions for a valid or complete marriage in the eyes of God were not present at the time of marriage.

The Church believes that marriage involves many elements, all of which are important for it to be valid or complete in the eyes of God. The conditions for a valid marriage concern a person's freedom to marry, their readiness to make a marriage commitment, their understanding of – indeed their very capacity to understand and live out – what marriage involves, their openness to having children, the proper process for witnessing a marriage, and so on.

In the case of a marriage between two Christians, there are certain additional requirements regarding how the marriage is celebrated. Only if all these aspects are fulfilled will the marriage be a valid one.[15]

What is the legal definition of "separation"?

"One or both of the spouses form the intention to sever or not to resume the marital relationship and act on that intention, or alternatively act as if the marital relationship has been severed."[16]

We've been married for less than two years. Can we get divorced?

Yes, subject to the following:

1. You and your partner have considered getting back together with the assistance of an appropriate professional through counselling (the legislation outlines who is an appropriate professional) or

2. If you haven't attended counselling, then with the court's permission *before* you apply for divorce.

Test your knowledge of this chapter by accessing our interactive book at deanpublishing.com/siobhanmullins

7

DIVORCE

Guy Advice

I guess the proudest moment for me was I didn't just sit back and cry. I moved forward, restarted my business, and went back to contracting like I always wanted to do but was never able to because of her. Like, she had a fear that it would go wrong. And literally, I just haven't looked back. I've been taking calculated risks and just going with it. And that's what I want. I'll listen to people's advice but at the same time, I'm just doing what I want. And I guess in my mind, I'm proud of myself for that because I never did it then – she didn't want me to. I just sort of went with the flow. So, now I'm doing what I want.

CHAPTER 8

Thinking Ahead

8

THINKING AHEAD

INTRODUCTION

CHECKLIST

Who needs to be provided with your updated personal contact information?

Who do you need or want to tell that you and your partner have separated?

What passwords, if any, need to be updated?

What precautionary interim financial steps do you need to take?

What other matters do you need to consider?

What documents do you need to store safely?

What financial documents do you need to gather?

8

THINKING AHEAD

INTRODUCTION

Given that you're in the process of – or already – separating, there are personal admin matters that you'll need to turn your attention towards sorting. You might want or need to do this now or later – whether in the lead-up to making your financial separation agreement official, just after, or even before or just after getting divorced (if relevant to you).

Note that the below is an informational checklist only and isn't exhaustive. It's a checklist designed to help you think ahead.

CHECKLIST

Who needs to be provided with your updated personal contact information?

☐ Superannuation fund(s)

☐ Employer

☐ MyGov (for Medicare, ATO and the like)

☐ Centrelink

☐ Bank(s) for all bank accounts, loans, and credit cards

☐ Motor vehicle registry (for vehicle registration purposes and updating your driver's licence – change of address)

☐ Any other required government agency (for example, immigration, public housing, DVA including for the purpose of updating any DVA, healthcare or pensioner's card details)

☐ Vehicle insurer

☐ Land titles (for rates notices)

☐ Utility service providers (for electricity, water and gas)

☐ PayPal

☐ ASIC (for any company shares/office holdings)

- [ ] Buy-now-pay-later solutions (Zip Pay, Afterpay, Splitit)

- [ ] Insurance providers (income protection, life, trauma, TPD, home and contents, and building insurances)

- [ ] Your PO box provider/Australia Post parcel locker details

- [ ] Update your mobile phone emergency contacts list

- [ ] Any other organisation or friend or family who require your next of kin details

Who do you need or want to tell that you and your partner have separated?

The decision about who and when you tell that you and your partner have separated is entirely yours.

- [ ] The bank
- [ ] Your employer
- [ ] Your GP
- [ ] Your counsellor
- [ ] Your accountant
- [ ] Your financial advisor/planner
- [ ] The security vetting agency (if relevant)

- ☐ The real estate agent (if renting)
- ☐ Your child's day care provider or school
- ☐ Your estate planning lawyer
- ☐ Your commercial lawyer (if applicable)
- ☐ Department of Home Affairs (if relevant)

What passwords, if any, need to be updated?

- ☐ Your computer password
- ☐ Apple ID
- ☐ Your mobile phone password
- ☐ Any iPads or tablet device passwords
- ☐ Your MyGov password
- ☐ Your email
- ☐ Your LastPass logon password
- ☐ Your social media (Facebook, Instagram, Snapchat, TikTok, WhatsApp, Signal)
- ☐ Any loyalty memberships (Qantas Frequent Flyer, Virgin Velocity, Emirates, Uber, Woolworths, Coles, Labour Club)
- ☐ Your share portfolio account password

☐ Your superannuation fund logon

☐ Your credit card pin(s)

☐ Your bank account pin(s)

☐ Any online banking passwords

What precautionary interim financial steps do you need to take?

(Be sure to read pages 18 and 19, and Chapter 9 before deciding firmly on whether to action the below).

☐ Telling the bank you're separated, with a view of freezing all accounts and/or requiring joint signatories to withdraw or transfer funds altogether or over a certain limit

☐ Removing any secondary cardholders for any credit or debit cards

☐ Removing saved passwords/personal information from your website browser(s)

What other matters do you need to consider?

Superannuation

☐ Nominate/consider updating your superannuation death beneficiary nomination(s)

☐ Consider getting advice as to the impact of any

superannuation split or proposed superannuation split and how to rebuild your super

☐ If you have a defined benefit superannuation interest, you'll need to consider getting a family law valuation. Use the QR code below for suggested information on getting your defined benefit superannuation valued.

Insurances

☐ Get/review your income protection insurance policy

☐ Get/review your life insurance policy and any nominated beneficiaries

☐ Get/review your private health insurance policy
   ◦ If you intend to remove your partner from the health insurance policy, consider whether this needs to be done immediately, can be delayed or if you'll tell her. There are waiting periods for health insurance so if you remove your partner from the private health insurance policy, it would be kind to tell her.
   ◦ If your partner is the policy holder, it might be an idea to have a conversation with her about whether you remain on the existing policy or get your own.

☐ Get/review trauma insurance

☐ Get/review temporary and permanent disability insurance – and be sure to review the amount of insurance you're covered for

---

A financial planner once told me that he bought his home off a gentleman in his late 40s – let's call him Todd. Todd had income protection, TPD and trauma insurance. He was involved in a motorbike accident that left him permanently disabled, bound to a wheelchair. He received a trauma lump sum payout, which he and his wife used to modify their home to accommodate his wheelchair. Todd also received a TPD payout, which meant his wife could take time off work and be beside him during the three months that he was in hospital. The TPD payout also covered Todd's rehab/physio costs.

Todd was unable to return to his former occupation because of his disabilities. Fortunately, because he had income protection insurance for the rest of his working life, he continued to receive income at a percentage of his previous salary. This assisted in paying for Todd's day-to-day expenses and enabled him to study and become a graphic designer. I can't drive home enough the importance of you getting your insurances right, especially if you've got children.

☐ Your will, enduring powers of attorney and guardianship

☐ Updating your will and estate plan on an interim basis pending your financial split being resolved and pending being divorced (if relevant)

☐ Get a/review/revoke any enduring powers of attorney that you may have (health and property) appointing your partner

8
THINKING AHEAD

☐ Get a/review your will

☐ Consider guardianship matters – that is, if you were to die whilst your children are under 18 years, then whose care they'd go into

☐ Review any organ and tissue donations you may have signed up for

What documents do you need to store safely?

☐ Your original birth certificate and passport

☐ Your passport

☐ Your child's/children's passports

☐ Any change of name certificates for yourself

What financial documents do you need to gather?

Please note that the below isn't an exhaustive list.

☐ Copies of documents relating to cost base of assets potentially attracting capital gains tax (for example shares, cryptocurrencies, ETFs, or investment properties)

☐ Bank transaction statements for all accounts, credit cards and personal loans 12 months before separation to date

- [ ] Hire purchase and lease agreements, including the current payout figure (as at or close to the date of separation payout figure and current)

- [ ] Superannuation member statements (as at or close to the date of separation payout figure and current)

- [ ] Cryptocurrency details – amount possessed and balance (as at or close to the date of separation payout figure and current)

- [ ] Share statements identifying the number of shares owned (as at or close to the date of separation payout figure and current)

- [ ] Exchange-traded funds, identifying the investments, including units owned and value (as at or close to the date of separation payout figure and current)

- [ ] Tax returns and notices of assessment for the last three financial years

- [ ] If you've got excess funds in any utilities accounts, then identifying the credit balance

- [ ] Appraisals for all real estate and vehicles, including motorbikes, trailers and caravans

- [ ] If you've got a company, an ASIC company search, a copy of the constitution, financials for the last three financial years

- [ ] If you've got a trust, a copy of the deed and financials for the last three years

8

THINKING AHEAD

☐ If you've got a self-managed superannuation fund (SMSF), then a copy the deed, financials for the last three financial years, a copy of the title searches for all property owned by the SMSF, a recent statement of the SMSF's share portfolio (if relevant), if there is a corporate trustee, then a copy of the constitution, the trustee's ABN, and if there is a limited borrowing recourse, then documents in relation to any bare trustee deed and constitution.

CHAPTER 9

Getting to an Agreement

9 GETTING TO AN AGREEMENT

INTRODUCTION
OPTIONS TO AGREE
MAKING THE AGREEMENT OFFICIAL

9

GETTING TO AN AGREEMENT

INTRODUCTION

Getting to an agreement doesn't just happen naturally. It requires you and your partner to work together.

9 OPTIONS TO AGREE

There are many process options to help you and your partner come to a separation agreement or achieve a resolution that doesn't involve you going to court.

	Relevant matters	Who is it for?	What's involved?
DIY	Parenting Financial Child support Maintenance	Couples who have great communication and realistic expectations regarding appropriate outcomes	You and your partner communicate with one another directly and reach an agreement. I often suggest to parents that if they need it, seeing a child psychologist together can help to understand their child's developmental needs better, using that information to help them agree on an appropriate parenting arrangement.
Mediation	Parenting Financial Child support Maintenance	Couples who have realistic expectations and need some help with communication	You and your partner participate in meetings with a mediator (an independent third person) who helps you to communicate and constructively work towards reaching an agreement together.
Lawyer-mediation	Parenting Financial Child support Maintenance	Couples with some complexity to their finances or who have poor communication, or the dynamics of their relationship require lawyer involvement to assist and advise, but they still want to participate in mediation.	You, your partner, and your lawyers participate in meetings with a mediator.

Child-inclusive mediation	Parenting	Couples who don't need help resolving their financial split and who are focused on prioritising and better understanding their child's needs (where their child is upper-primary school age plus)	A child expert interviews your child and provides feedback to a mediator regarding your child's views. Then, the mediator meets with you and your partner to share your child's views and feedback to inform your parenting agreement.
Parenting coordination	Parenting Child support	Couples who have communication difficulties and need help to better co-parent with their partner	You and your partner engage a parenting coordinator (PC), being a coach, who works with you both. The PC supports you in effectively co-parenting your kids with advice, support, information, and dispute resolution help.
Collaborative family law	Parenting Financial Child support Maintenance	Couples who have some complexity to their finances or sensitive relationship dynamics and can afford ongoing lawyer involvement	You and your partner each engage a collaboratively trained family lawyer to work with you. Then, through a series of four-way meetings, you negotiate from an interests-based position (versus a strict legal entitlements position) to reach an agreement together.
Lawyer-letter writing	Parenting Financial Child support Maintenance	Couples whose communication has broken down or one or both people don't have realistic expectations about appropriate outcomes	You or your partner engage a lawyer to act on your behalf. That lawyer provides information to the other person (or their lawyer) and negotiates regarding all offers about unresolved matters on their client's behalf, for example, financial, parenting, child support, and maintenance.
Arbitration	Parenting Financial Maintenance	Couples whose communication has broken down, who want a faster and more affordable legally binding outcome than going to court	You and your partner engage a qualified arbitrator (a qualified decision-maker) to decide on the division of your financial split, parenting, maintenance and child support for you. The arbitrator's decision is legally binding.

MAKING THE AGREEMENT OFFICIAL

Parenting

There are only two ways you can make your parenting agreement official – official meaning recognised as a legal agreement. The two different ways are a parenting plan and a parenting consent order.

There's no legal requirement to make your parenting agreement official, but there can certainly be some benefits in doing so:

- Peace of mind – a shared mutual understanding of your agreement, expectations, and obligations

- Clarity and assurance – confidence in your ability to plan and set a routine for your child

- Better communication – improved and reduced communication with your partner because the agreement is clear on what's expected to happen

- Life made easier – a documented agreement can help with Centrelink, child support, your child's school/day care, their GP and the like, who may ask for written confirmation of the agreement

The below table identifies the major differences between the two different agreement types:

	Parenting Plan	Parenting Consent Order
Legally recognised	Yes	Yes
Binding & enforceable	No	Yes
Legal advice required	No – optional	No – optional
Court approval required	No	Yes
Lasts until child is 18 years	Yes, if by choice	Yes
Can easily be reviewed regularly	Yes	No
Can be updated/changed easily	Yes	No
Can deal with child support	Yes	No

Interested in making your parenting agreement official in a parenting plan? Scan the QR code to be taken to our resource page, where you can DIY your parenting plan.

9 Maintenance

For some people, maintenance is not going to be relevant because either:

- Each person has little to no buffer between their financial commitments and their income, or

- Each person can support themselves with their income, and they don't require maintenance.

Even if a couple has made their financial separation agreement official, if there's no official maintenance agreement, a person can seek that their partner pay maintenance. Divorced couples have 12 months from the date of their divorce to seek maintenance, and de facto couples have two years from the date of their separation.

If you and your partner did want to make your agreement about maintenance official – either stating that you won't seek it from one another or there is maintenance to be paid for a period – you can do so as follows:

	Financial Consent Order (FCO)	Binding Financial Agreement (BFA)
Legally recognised	Yes	Yes
Binding & enforceable	Yes	Yes
Legal advice required	No – optional	Yes
Court approval required	Yes	No
Can deal with maintenance	Yes	Yes
Can stop a person altogether seeking maintenance	No	Yes
Can deal with the financial split at the same time as maintenance	Yes	Yes

A judge could require maintenance to be paid by a person even if a BFA documents an agreement that nil maintenance is payable. What's relevant to this is if you or your partner, when entering into the BFA, were unable to support yourself without an income-tested pension, allowance or benefit.

9

Your financial split (property settlement)

There are only two ways to make your financial separation agreement official, that is legal, binding, and enforceable: a binding financial agreement (BFA) and a financial consent order (FCO). Paper napkin agreements, signed pieces of paper, emails, deeds, and statutory declarations don't cut the mustard.

For a BFA, you must involve a lawyer; there's no way around this requirement because you need legal advice. For an FCO, I'd say 99.9999 percent of people need legal help – not necessarily advice, as that isn't a requirement for an FCO – but legal help when it comes to the paperwork to ensure the calculations are all correct and the legalese is correctly and appropriately drafted.

	Financial Consent Order	Binding Financial Agreement
Legally recognised	Yes	Yes
Binding & enforceable	Yes	Yes
Legal advice required	No – optional	Yes
Court approval required	Yes	No
Can deal with maintenance	Yes	Yes
Stamp duty concessions available on transfer of some assets	Yes	Yes
Capital gains tax rollover relief available on the transfer of some assets	Yes	Yes
Can deal with maintenance at the same time as the financial split	Yes	Yes
Stops a person altogether seeking maintenance	No	Yes

9 Child support

Depending on your and your partner's level of trust for one another and your respective commitments to financially support your children, you may choose to make your child support agreement official in one of three ways: parenting plan, limited child support agreement or binding child support agreement.

Some parents want a degree of certainty when it comes to what they can expect to pay or receive in child support, so they may go for the longer-term option, being a binding child support agreement.

A breakdown of the major differences between the three options is provided opposite.

Another alternative is to apply to the court for child support departure orders. This involves an application to the court and requires a court order to depart from a child support assessment. This is complicated to go into and if it is something that you feel is relevant to you, get legal advice from an experienced family lawyer.

Want to find out more about parenting and child support? Get access to our Parenting & Child Support Bundle by scanning the QR code.

	Parenting Plan	Limited Child Support Agreement	Binding Child Support Agreement
Legally recognised	Yes	Yes	Yes
Binding & enforceable	No – but relevant to a child support reassessment	Yes – subject to the terms	Yes – subject to the terms
Registered with the Child Support Agency	No – optional	Yes, best practice	Yes, best practice
Requires a child support assessment	No	Yes	No (unless there's a lump sum child support payment forming part of the agreement)
Duration	As long as plan says	For three years only	Until child is 18 years
Legal advice required	No	No	Yes
Can be reviewed regularly & easily	Yes	No	No
Can be updated/ changed easily	Yes	No	No

Guys' Experience

In putting together this book, I met with and interviewed about ten men, whom I'd worked with and who'd separated and reached a separation agreement with their partners. Below is a compilation of the best advice, thought processes and experiences they shared with me.

What contributed to the separation?

We'd always have arguments. So, the biggest driver, like, the biggest wedge that happened towards the end was every time I'd go to work, we'd argue that day or the night before. So, we would always leave arguing, or I would always leave arguing. And it would just be over stupid shit. Nothing special at all. We could just never ... she could never take criticism, so if I'd say that something's not right, she couldn't take criticism. But yeah, I don't know. That's what really started driving it. It was the fact that I'd go to work fighting every time.

– Steve

Months later she sent me this whole big "I'm sorry" message type thing, basically apologised for everything that happened. And she sort of said, "How could I expect you to love me when I couldn't even love and respect myself?" A big hurdle we had in our relationship was, it wouldn't matter how many times I'd tell her that she was good looking or she was beautiful, whatever, she would never accept that within herself. She always said that she wasn't good enough. I don't know, she's funny, gorgeous and unbelievable.

– Andrew

For me to get over that as a guy, you know, catching them in the act was ... So that's where I could've been that other person, been bitter, nasty and all of that. And, you know, I probably was inside, but outside I had to keep it together for my girls. I grew up in a volatile upbringing. She grew up in a volatile upbringing. I didn't want to become that person. If I stayed, I probably would've become that person.
– Chris

Advice on coping

Get the professional help because you may turn to comfort things such as alcohol, food, drugs, whatever. You need to take hold of where you're at and make good decisions for your future and your children's future. It's so hard to just say, "Fuck it all" and move on. There's nothing wrong with a fuck it all attitude, but you need to let those emotions go, don't self-destruct.

– Tim

I've got enough friends and people around me to say, "Well, why don't you go talk to this person? Why don't you talk to this doctor?" Doctors are good. Doctors are probably your first point to talk to. So don't go through this emotionally, not dealing with things. They can help you with depression, anxiety, whatever it is that you may be going through.

– Glen

I hate to say it, but most counsellors are female, which is, from a male perspective, not always good because they don't quite see things the same way. They understand the brain and how it works, and they understand the theory side of how it works, but they don't always understand the emotional side of a male head. I've only had one male counsellor, and the rest were ladies. Some of the ladies were great, but that one guy that I spoke to, he was awesome because he was a stepdad as well, similar sort of environment to me. He had one separation himself that he shared with me, which I thought usually they don't, but he was quite open to share that with me at the time. So yeah, I found him very helpful. I do think male counsellors are better for males, generally speaking.

– Rob

Males are not good at communicating and speaking to each other. It's more, "Let's have a beer." "Let's go fishing." We don't talk about things, we're just there. I found most of my male friends were good to just ease the pressure and have a laugh but not talk about anything serious. I've got a lot of girly friends, and I found them better for that side of things. Whereas the males were good just to relieve pressure.

– Steve

I'd probably feel a little bit uncomfortable talking deeply with most of my male friends. I'm not going to cry on their shoulder. It's just not me. Whereas a girl, yeah, I'll cry on their shoulder any day of the week. It's just who I am, and I think most guys are similar to that. Yeah, most males are. We're just different. We won't particularly talk to each other about stuff. It's probably why I've got more female friends than male friends.

– Mitch

Lessons learnt

You work out, "Okay, this is cool. This is not cool. This is where I need to improve and grow and develop and all that." That's what my personal experience has been with it.
– Jacob

I guess I think I should have opened up to somebody earlier. I should have listened to my partner when she was crying out for help, and I ignored it. I guess you could say it wasn't an obvious cry, it was a ... Yeah, the other person was crying out for attention or whatever, and I guess I was so caught up in my own life and work, and I guess I regret that. I guess I look at things, everything in life happens for a reason. I don't know if what happened and what I chose to do was for the right reason. I think I was just, one, caught up in my own world, and two, I was very sad, and I didn't talk to anyone about it.

– Jason

I felt that I needed to do what I was doing to let us move forward and give us everything I thought we wanted. So, I thought by doing what I was doing, it was a good thing, but all it did was drive us apart. Yeah, working the hours and not being home. And when I was home, I'd then work more, and then not wanting to be involved, and yeah, that.

– Andrew

I honestly believe if I would have quit my job and we kept going to counselling, we would have been fine. We would have worked together fine. It was just that I was never home, and that's what she wanted. We still would have had a good life, we just would have been together more. I would have got there eventually. I'm doing it now. I don't have enough time for it, but I'm doing it.
– Chris

What's life like now?

I've separated three times, and I think each time I was, it's going to sound terrible, but I really enjoyed a bit of freedom. A bit of me time, not so much freedom. It's more me time to think about who I want to be, where I want to go, do I want to leave town? Not that I ever did, but I could think about those options for me as a person and do what I wanted to do as opposed to what we wanted to do. So that was a bit of a selfish thing, I have to agree with that.

– Rob

As you're going through the emotional side of things, there's still the positives of, well, okay, I can go watch that movie with my mates and I don't have to ask permission. You don't have to ask permission for things that you want to do. I just go and do it, which is essentially very refreshing.

– Michael

I know I've since found someone who's just going to be the best person for me, but time will tell.

– Mitch

It's hard because you did know someone for so long, and I guess I moved on really quick, you compare that person. It's very easy to compare somebody to somebody else when you're used to something, you know what I mean?

– Jason

I talk a lot these days. I give a lot of positive and negative feedback. I think it's great. My new partner and I have definitely had our recent issues. I just find she's a little bit slack and lazy at things, and that's not how I like it. You know? And I make sure I tell her. Maybe I should keep things to myself sometimes, but I feel people need to know. And I definitely do try and talk about stuff, even though sometimes I don't want to. I definitely do.

– Andrew

Conclusion

Thank you for the opportunity to write this book for you. It's a book I've known needed to be written for many years because the hurdle of "what now," which you're confronted with after separating, can be so easily solved with the answers and practical information this book provides.

The Guys' Guide to Divorce & Separation has been about giving you perspective, understanding, insight and awareness for your situation, including your and your partner's headspace, emotions, fears, and goals.

Having read the chapters, you should now have:

- Clarity on what needs to be sorted out as part of your separation

- An awareness of important time limits

- Answers to many of your questions

- An understanding as to the importance of you looking after yourself physically and mentally

- An appreciation for what gets considered to determine appropriate legal outcomes for financial splits, child support, maintenance, and parenting after a couple separates

- A clear understanding of the different ways you and your partner can engage to reach agreement together

- An understanding of your options to making your separation agreements official

- An understanding of the different ways to communicate with your partner, including some of the pros and cons behind choosing one way over others

- Some insights into your partner's thoughts and behaviours

I hope to leave you feeling inspired to work with your partner so you can go your separate ways, but together.

And on that note, you've now had the opportunity to read through *The Guys' Guide to Divorce & Separation* and have your questions answered. What about giving your partner the same opportunity by giving her this book? I've included a note to her introducing this book's purpose.

Consider sharing this book with your partner and draw her attention to the "Note for Her" on pages 210–211.

I wish you every success going forward in life.
Siobhan

Note for Her

Hello partner,

I write this note to introduce myself and explain the purpose behind this book.

My name is Siobhan (pronounced "Sh-vaughn"), and I'm a collaboratively trained family lawyer.

I own a small business called Separate Together, which is best known for making the complexity and anxiety of separating simple so couples can achieve the very best outcomes for themselves and their families. Our resources help couples work together to reach parenting, child support and financial separation agreements, where we can then assist to prepare the paperwork to make it all official.

Enough about me.

You might be wondering, "Why would a female family lawyer write a book specifically to help separating men? Is she pro-men and anti-women? Why wouldn't she write a book that's for men *and* women who are separating?"

I have written this book specifically targeting a male reader because, compared to men, women are generally better at seeking support from others and getting advice. We (females) tend to talk about our problems and worries with our friends, families, mums, and/or in online forums. It's through sharing with others that we get a sense of perspective, a reality check, reassurance that we're doing the right thing, in addition to feeling emotionally supported. We seek out the correct information and proper answers to our questions by getting advice.

Guys don't seem to have that same sort of tendency to share problems and worries with friends. And for some guys, their support network largely consists of their partner's friends' husbands and their partner's extended family. That support network can fall away during a separation.

Men already have a greater risk of suicide and mental health issues than women. This risk is increased when men experience a breakdown in their relationship and is further compounded by the absence of emotional support and proper help. I believe more must be done to draw attention to men's mental health and the need for men to manage and prioritise it. The guy advice and insights included in this book and chapter two, "Looking after You," seek to do just that.

In not getting perspective, a reality check, correct information and proper answers, guys are at a disadvantage. Without a framework, some guiding principles, practical information, and answers, the reality is that neither you or your partner can constructively engage in discussions about your child's care arrangements, their financial support, or what an appropriate financial split looks like.

By writing this book with a title that's male-specific, I have given your partner a resource that he feels is for "him." He's more inclined to pick it up off the shelf, read it, be open to accepting the information and answers within, and then subsequently sharing it with you. The beauty of this book, though, is that the questions and answers are ones that you will likely have too, so read away!

In answer to those other two questions, I am pro whatever gender a person identifies with, and I *have* previously written a book for men and women who are separating. It's called *Splitting Up Together: The How-To Handbook for an AMICABLE Divorce*, which breaks down my AMICABLE methodology to explain from start to finish what's involved in separating, reaching an agreement, and making it official.

In writing this book, I've sought to help your partner first, which in turn helps you and, consequently, your whole family.

I wish you every success in working with your partner to achieve the very best outcome for you and your family. Siobhan.

About the Author

Siobhan Mullins was never popular at school; she was always a bit different from her peers. Her mum called it "unique."

After experiencing some trauma in her teen years, a passion for helping people was sparked, leading her to begin studying social work at university. However, after realising that her studies didn't activate her analytical mind, Siobhan switched to studying social science in justice studies. She finished her first degree and, after that, completed a law degree.

With an interest in education, kids, and the idea of regular holidays, as a child, Siobhan wanted to become a teacher. Now her passion in practicing law is to help people through, and educate them about, the separation process in a unique and different way.

You need only look at what Siobhan has built with Separate Together to recognise that one of her greatest strengths is her ability to empathise. Her other significant strength is her ability to create and build content, systems and processes that meaningfully solve and satisfy others' needs.

Siobhan has won awards for her innovation in law and is the brains behind Separate Together, a multi-award-winning family law firm, named as one of Australia's most innovative firms, reimagining the business of law.

Notes

NOTES

NOTES

NOTES

ENDNOTES

1 Domestic Violence Victoria and Domestic Violence Resource Centre Victoria, *Submission 147*, p. 34.

2 Women's Safety NSW, *Submission 150.1: Attachment 1*, p. 6.

3 Youth Affairs Council of South Australia (YACSA), *Submission 112*, p. 6.

4 Australian Government 2016, *Family Law Act 1975*, Canberra, viewed 29 June 2022, https://www.legislation.gov.au/Details/C2016C01106.

5 Australian Bureau of Statistics 2013, *Defining the Data Challenge for Family, Domestic and Sexual Violence*, viewed 29 June 2022, https://www.abs.gov.au/statistics/people/crime-and-justice/defining-data-challenge-family-domestic-and-sexual-violence/latest-release.

6 Cook, B, David, F & Grant, A 2001, *Sexual Violence in Australia*, Australian Institute of Criminology, Canberra, viewed 29 June 2022, https://www.aic.gov.au/sites/default/files/2020-05/rpp036.pdf.

7 Australian Government 2016, *Family Law Act 1975*, Canberra, viewed 29 June 2022, https://www.legislation.gov.au/Details/C2016C01106.

8 Australian Institute of Family Studies 2019, *Parenting Arrangements after Separation*, report, Australian Institute of Family Studies, Melbourne, viewed 25 July 2022, https://aifs.gov.au/sites/default/files/publication-documents/1910_parenting_arrangements_after_separation.pdf.

9 Kubler-Ross, E & Kessler, D 2005, *On Grief and Grieving: Finding the Meaning of Grief Through the Five Stages of Loss*, Scribner, New York City.

10 Barry, JA & Liddon, L 2020, 'Child Contact Problems and Family Court Issues Are Related to Chronic Mental Health Problems for Men Following Family Breakdown', *Psychreg Journal of Psychology*, vol 4, no 3, pp 57-66, viewed 29 June 2022, https://discovery.ucl.ac.uk/id/eprint/10118128/1/barry-liddon-57-66.pdf.

11 Australian Bureau of Statistics 2021, *Causes of Death, Australia*, viewed 29 June 2022, https://www.abs.gov.au/statistics/health/causes-death/causes-death-australia/latest-release#intentional-self-harm-deaths-suicide-in-australia.

12 Australian Bureau of Statistics 2021, *Marriages and Divorces, Australia*, viewed 29 June 2022, https://www.abs.gov.au/statistics/people/people-and-communities/marriages-and-divorces-australia/latest-release.

13 American Psychological Association 2018, *Stress Effects on the Body*, viewed 29 June 2022, https://www.apa.org/topics/stress/body.

14 Mehrabian, A 1981, *Silent Messages: Implicit Communication of Emotions and Attitudes*, 2nd edn, Wadsworth Publishing Co Inc.

15 Catholic Australia, *How Can the Church Declare That Some Marriages Are Invalid and the Couple Free to Marry Again?*, viewed 29 June 2022, https://www.catholicaustralia.com.au/the-sacraments/divorce/183.

16 Family Court of Australia, *Pavey, T.G. and Pavey, J.P. [1976] FamCA 36; (1976) FLC 90-051 (15 June 1976)*, viewed 29 June 2022, http://www8.austlii.edu.au/cgi-bin/viewdoc/au/cases/cth/FamCA/1976/36.html.

www.ingramcontent.com/pod-product-compliance
Lightning Source LLC
Chambersburg PA
CBHW070423120526
44590CB00014B/1514